100+ Tips and Tricks for Success in Language Learning

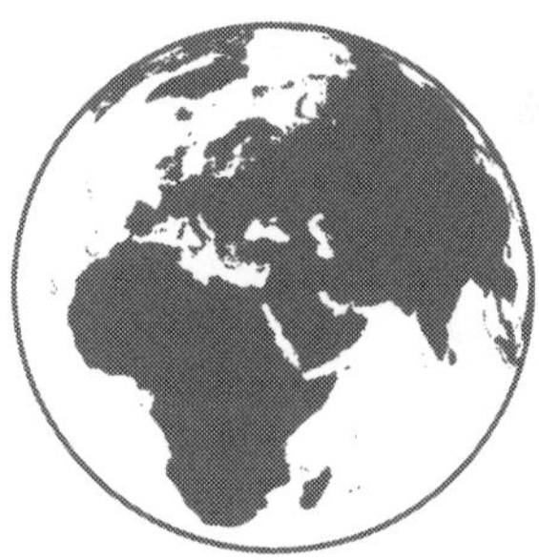

Felicity O'Dell and Patricia Pullin

Published by O'Dell & Pullin

The URLs are accurate at the time of writing but are subject to change.

First published 2020

ISBN: 978 1 8382311 0 1 paperback

ISBN: 978 1 8382311 1 8 e-book

Design by Bob Swan at Blue Dog Design Studio
Typeset in Guardi
Illustrations by Peter Bull Art Studio
Artwork by Greg Orrom Swan
Printed by Amazon

Contents

D Learning words 79

E Getting to grips with grammar 111

F Improving understanding 139

Introduction

Have you ever admired people who are at ease in a foreign language, or even several? Maybe you've already tried to learn another language, perhaps at school, but you didn't manage to reach a level where you could really use the language. Or, perhaps you've always wanted to learn a foreign language, but never got round to it.

Whatever your previous experience or current aims, this book unlocks the secrets of language learning, making language learning fun and helping you to become a successful language learner. In ten sections, we outline a wide range of tips and tricks that will assist you in planning and carrying through your language learning project to achieve your own individual aims, be they ordering a coffee in Paris or Shanghai, giving a presentation at a conference or reading a novel in your chosen language.

The tips we present in the book will be useful both for people who are new to language learning and for those who have already learnt one or more foreign languages and want to learn another; they will also help people who are just starting to learn their target language as well as those who have already made considerable progress.

Anyone anywhere can learn a foreign language. No special ability is required. International footballers soon learn what they need when they relocate to play for a foreign team. Migrants have always moved to other countries to find work when it's scarce at home and they usually master as much of the language as they require. If you're really motivated to learn, then you can do it.

While learning a language inevitably still requires effort, in some ways it's easier than it ever used to be. In our digital world, we can access media and make contact with people all over the world, whatever the language we want to practise. This means that we can experience our target language wherever we are in the world. What's more, it's become much easier to tailor what we do to suit our own individual interests and needs and this generally serves to make our learning more effective.

There are many reasons why learning a language is worthwhile. Some specialists believe that having even some knowledge of a second language is good for the brain. It appears to improve the ability to multitask, to empathise and even to stave off mental decline in old age. Language learning opens doors: professional, cultural and personal; sharpens our brains and opens our minds. Learning a new language may be the beginning of a new chapter in your life and perhaps even a series of adventures!

Suggestions for how to use the book

Few people read non-fiction books from cover to cover, so we'd like to give you some hints as to how to get the best out of this book.

We suggest you start by looking through the contents of the first two sections, A *Making plans* and B *Ways of learning,* and reading the tips that strike you as being the most useful to you immediately. You can always go back to the other tips later. These two sections cover points that are important to anyone wishing to learn a foreign language. Then you can work through the other sections in any order that suits you.

Section C, *Focusing on things you're (almost) sure to need,* is most relevant for those of you who are starting a new language from scratch perhaps with a view to using it for travel purposes. Section D, *Learning words,* is of core importance as without vocabulary there would be no language! Section E, *Getting to grips with grammar,* focuses on aspects of grammar learning while F, *Improving understanding,* looks at listening to and reading real-life materials in your target language. Section G, *Sounding good,* deals with pronunciation and H, *Progressing and making learning stick,* considers a number of ways of helping you to make steady progress and stick at it. Section I, *Communicating in different cultures,* investigates aspects of communication that vary from one culture to another. This section can help you to benefit from contact with people from other cultures who speak your target language, and also to avoid pitfalls when you have such contact. Finally, we hope you will enjoy dipping into the last section, *Tips from successful language learners,* for inspiration, as it consists of a set of case studies relating to a variety of people who have achieved success in language learning.

And what about the tips and tricks in the title? Well, in each section we outline a number of tips and tricks. These are based on our experience both as teachers and learners and our training as language teachers. After each set of tips we hand over to you with an activity inviting you to apply these ideas to your own situation. We have provided space in the book for you to deal with the exercises and write your answers. You might also like to buy an exercise book or set up a digital file to make additional notes and build on some of the exercises.

Enjoy the book! We wish you every success in your learning and the new adventures it may lead to.

A Making plans

All men's well-being depends on two things; one is the right choice of target, of the end to which actions should tend, the other lies in finding the actions that lead to that end.

Aristotle (384–322 BCE): *The Politics*

When it comes to learning a language, as with many things in life, you're much more likely to succeed if you first make a plan. A plan ensures you choose the right target or goal, as Aristotle suggested millennia ago, and the appropriate means to achieve it.

The choice of target in this case includes which language you want or need to study and how good you want or need to be at understanding, speaking, reading and writing it. Your starting point or level of knowledge and the context in which you will be learning will also be important factors in planning your learning, as well as the way you like to learn.

Once you have outlined these points, you can then set a global aim and find the actions Aristotle mentions to help you achieve this aim. You will need to break your overall aim down into a series of micro-aims that are achievable and measurable. We will show you how to work towards them using proven approaches to language learning that also allow you to experiment with different ways of learning. This will help you to find the best approach for you, one that fits your lifestyle and the way you like to learn.

Aims of this section

The tips in this section show you how to:

- clarify your reasons for learning a language
- decide which language to study
- set a global aim in terms of your starting point and what you want to be able to do in the language
- break down the global aim into a series of micro-aims
- identify learning activities to work towards your micro-aims
- draw up an individual learning plan with regular learning slots and activities that fit in with your lifestyle
- understand how to review and measure your progress and enjoy rewards when you reach your goals.

The section also considers the nature of language learning, how people learn languages, and what research tells us about successful language learners.

1 Fathom your reasons

Research shows that motivation and needs are two of the key factors that lead to success in language learning. So before you start planning your language learning, you should have a clear idea of why you want to learn a foreign language. In some cases, the decision may not be yours, such as when a new job requires new language skills. But working out your reasons for learning a language and choosing the 'right' language will help you to set clear and achievable aims and make language learning more enjoyable and successful.

So why do people learn foreign languages? Here are some of the reasons. See if you can identify with one or more of them and make some notes to help you with your planning.

Travel – travelling the world at any age is stimulating and being able to use local languages enriches the experience. You don't need a high level of language skill to be able to communicate with local people, but you can still get insights into local cultures and make new friends if you have some ability to use their language.

Education – whether you're doing an apprenticeship or studying at university, exchange programmes abound. Studying in another country and language can be challenging, but apart from learning to live in another culture, you may also build up a network of lifetime friends and possible later professional contacts.

Work – having more than one language on your CV/résumé is a definite advantage for your career and can offer a range of opportunities not available to monolinguals.

Love – when we fall in love with someone from another country, it's natural to want to learn their language in order to be able to understand their culture and communicate with them and their family. Knowing another language or seeking out opportunities to learn and practise language can of course lead to meeting someone and falling in love!

Family and friends – some people are highly motivated to learn or improve a language spoken by their grandparents or other members of their own family. Learning languages, when it involves travelling and working in other countries, also naturally leads to meeting new people and making new friends. This of course then increases motivation to keep working on your language skills and enjoying using the language.

Culture – some people fall in love with a country's culture, its literature or simply its people and way of life. Language is an important key to understanding culture, and learning the language of a culture that you love, be it Chinese or Italian, can be a fascinating project.

Hobby – language learning can simply be a hobby. People who enjoy language learning often take courses, meeting other like-minded people and enjoying their company. Regular activities outside the class such as going to films in the chosen language or meeting for a coffee to practise speaking together can become part of an enjoyable routine.

Retirement – learning or brushing up your knowledge of a language helps to sharpen the brain. In fact, language learning is a form of mental gymnastics and some studies show that it's an ideal activity to keep your brain fit as you get older.

Over to you

What is your main reason for wanting to learn a language?

....

....

Or perhaps you have more than one reason:

....

....

....

....

....

What are the main benefits for you of learning this language?

....

....

....

....

....

....

2 Choose your language

You may have to learn a specific language as part of your studies, for your job, or because you're moving to another country. Or you may be able to choose the language yourself. If so, there are thousands of languages you could choose from.

Here, we identify a number of factors to help you decide which language to study.

1 Why do you want to learn a language?

You may want to learn for reasons connected with your work or your family background. Or it could be for travel purposes. If you're planning a trip, say to South America, then learning Spanish would be a good choice. Portuguese is spoken in Brazil, but Spanish is taught in many schools there, so you will often be able to use Spanish in Brazil too.

2 How many people speak the language of your choice?

Currently, the languages with the largest number of speakers are Mandarin Chinese, Spanish, English and Hindustani. A language that is widely spoken is also likely to be widely taught, so training materials and courses will be available and you can also find people to practise with.

3 How easy or difficult is the language likely to be for you?

If you have studied the language before, for example at school, even in the distant past, you will probably find it easier to recall and understand the basics than if you were starting from scratch in a new language. This will give you a head start.

How closely the language is related to your native language or other languages you already know can be a key factor. There are many websites that show how different languages are related to each other. So if your native language or another language you have studied is a Romance language, such as French, this will make learning related languages, for example Italian or Spanish, easier. This is largely because a lot of the vocabulary in these languages comes from the same roots and will be similar. Keeping things easy is more likely to result in your carrying on studying over time, which is essential to really learn a language.

If, on the other hand, you want to learn a language that isn't related to your language or languages you have already studied, the task will be more challenging. For speakers of European languages, learning Arabic, for example, involves learning a new script. For Asian languages such as Chinese or Japanese, learning to read and write involves memorising a lot of characters. While Chinese grammar may be more straightforward than that of many other languages, the tone system used in speaking, whereby one word can have different meanings depending on the way you pronounce it, can be difficult to master. Some people like such challenges more than others do.

The clearer your motivation and needs, the more successful you will be. But you also need to be realistic about the task you're taking on!

Over to you

Which language are you thinking about learning?

. . . .

Why do you want to learn this particular language?

. . . .

. . . .

. . . .

How many people speak the language?

. . . .

Where do they live?

. . . .

. . . .

Is the language related to your language?

. . . .

. . . .

. . . .

How easily can you find people to practise with?

. . . .

. . . .

. . . .

3 How good is 'good enough'?

You may feel you want to reach the highest level possible in your chosen language, or you may have simple aims based on limited needs in terms of what you need to do in the language.

If you're planning a walking holiday in Italy, you may want to learn basic language that can help you to understand menus and order meals in restaurants or enquire about accommodation. So long as you can make yourself understood, you will be happy. If, on the other hand, you need Italian for your job, your aims might have to be more ambitious. You may need to make presentations at specialist conferences. In this case, you will not only need to be able to deal competently with the presentations themselves, but also be able to answer follow-up questions. In addition, you should be able to make small talk at mealtimes and during social activities. Another area that could affect how high you need to aim or how good you need to be would be whether you're taking exams. This could be to advance in your career or for entry into another country where you intend to work or study. In such cases, you may need to reach a very high standard!

So 'good enough' may range from having just enough language to obtain food or drink on holiday to using the language at an advanced level in professional contexts. Or it may mean passing exams that test all your language skills and knowledge of grammar with tasks involving understanding and producing complex texts.

How good is 'good enough' may also depend on your attitude to language learning and use and how relaxed you are about life in general. For many language learners, what is most important is being able to understand others and be understood when they speak or write. For some, writing may be simple messages in emails or texts in which non-standard use doesn't matter or doesn't worry them, so long as the message is comprehensible. Others may wish to use more complex language and ensure that it's well structured and correct in terms of standard grammatical usage. The choice will probably also depend on the context. If you're working in the field of law, for example, precision is more likely to be important than in many other fields.

The time available for learning and the need to use the language as quickly as possible are also factors that may affect your attitudes to what is 'good enough'.

Over to you

How would you define 'good enough' in relation to your individual aims?

Is 'good enough' the same for you in speaking, listening, reading and writing? If not, how does it differ?

Are you a perfectionist or easy-going? How is this likely to affect your approach to learning?

4 Do you really need to write?

Most language courses cover all four of the language skills: the receptive skills of reading and listening and the productive skills of speaking and writing.

Writing can help fix new knowledge in your mind, but this can mean writing as little as a few short phrases or a sentence. But in terms of real communication, you may decide you don't need to write at all. For example, if you intend to communicate in the target language when travelling you will need to speak and understand others and also to read, but you may never need to write.

Whatever your needs, it's unlikely that you will be able to really communicate with others in writing, for example in emails, in the early stages of learning a language. This is simply because you will not yet have enough vocabulary or knowledge of the grammar to make your message clear. But when you begin to feel you're ready to write to other people, it doesn't matter if you make mistakes so long as the people you're addressing understand your message or can ask you to clarify it. Such messages should be brief, and this is an ideal way of beginning to write.

There are good reasons for avoiding writing long texts until you have reached a more advanced level. If you're writing in a class context and writing longer texts you will inevitably make mistakes and all the corrections can be demotivating.

But perhaps your specific aim is to learn to write or improve your writing in the language. This may be a requirement for your job, in which case identify exactly what you need to write in the target language, for example emails or reports. Find a coach or teacher who can help you to develop the necessary knowledge and skills. Get this person to help you work on real texts that you have to write and also teach you how to edit or correct them. You may find useful models in textbooks or online, or be able to use colleagues' written texts as models.

Some people like writing and this may be a reason to choose to write, even at lower levels. This is something we address later in the book in Tip 78 *Write to consolidate and extend your knowledge*.

Over to you

Do you really need to write in your target language now or can you wait?

If you need to write, what do you need to write?

Where can you find someone to help you with this?

Where can you find useful models for writing?

5 Identify your aims

How do you plan in everyday life? Are you someone who makes detailed plans and sticks to them, or do you prefer to have a rough outline and a lot of flexibility?

Whatever your approach to planning, we recommend you plan your language learning project systematically. This will help you maintain your motivation, enjoy learning the language and achieve your aims.

Setting a global goal

At this stage, you will have decided which language to learn and have an idea of what you wish to achieve or be able to do in the language as your end goal.

It's a good idea to write down your goal in one sentence and then review it regularly.

Here are three examples of global learning goals:

	Learner profile	**Target language**	**Starting level**	**Timeframe**	**Global aim**
1	Stay-at-home parent	French	Elementary	1 year 3–4 hours per week	To use everyday French on a family camping holiday in France, speaking with local people, shopping and taking part in local sporting activities
2	Manager	Russian	Rusty advanced	6 months 2–3 hours a week	To speak fluently with new Russian business partners and their families and write simple emails
3	Retiree	Survival Chinese	Beginner	1 year initially	To be able to use and understand basic language on future holidays in China

Over to you

To what extent does your situation resemble any of the examples in the table? Complete the table below with your own profile and global aim.

If you aren't a beginner in the language, you may need some help in assessing your initial level and how realistic your aims are in relation to the time you have, your level of motivation and lifestyle (you may need to be less ambitious!).

Learner profile	Target language	Starting level	Timeframe	Global aim

6 Draw up a plan

Once you have a clear overall goal in writing, an idea of the timeframe for your project and time available on a weekly basis, you can begin to break your goal down into a series of smaller goals. It's better to have micro-targets than one very ambitious aim you may never reach! You can then begin to identify learning activities to fit into your weekly schedule in working towards these aims.

Drawing up an individual learning plan will help you to map your path and to work regularly on the language. It will also give you opportunities to measure your progress, evaluate if the plan is working or needs adjustment and, importantly, enjoy rewards when you reach your goals.

Here are seven essential points to bear in mind when drawing up an individual language learning plan. The plan should be:

1 **Specific:** define your aim and the activities you're going to do.

2 **Relevant:** don't waste time on activities that aren't essential for your final goal.

3 **Realistic:** don't try to fit too much into the week or set yourself difficult, off-putting tasks.

4 **Regular:** budget regular time slots to maintain motivation and make real progress.

5 **Enjoyable:** include stimulating activities, at least most of the time!

6 **Flexible:** have a Plan B for very busy times – try to avoid dropping your learning completely.

7 **Measurable:** review your approach to learning and assess your progress regularly.

Over to you

Based on the seven points, make a few preliminary notes in relation to your own learning, before going on to look at planning in more detail in Tip 7 *Learning plans in practice*.

. . . .

. . . .

. . . .

. . . .

. . . .

. . . .

. . . .

. . . .

. . . .

7 Learning plans in practice

Look at the three sample plans that follow. Would any of these approaches suit you?

Sample plan 1

Learner profile	Target language	Starting level	Timeframe	Global aim
Stay-at-home parent	French	Elementary	1 year 3–4 hours per week	To use everyday French on a family camping holiday in France, speaking with local people, shopping and taking part in local sporting activities

This learner has chosen a weekly timetable for his learning plan. He learnt French at school, but never used it. He has decided to take a class one evening a week at a local college. After an entry test, he has been placed in an elementary class (A2)* with the aim of reaching lower-intermediate (B1)* over the year. The coursebook and workbook he has bought for his course have clear aims per chapter and will help him to reach his global goal over the year. The plan that follows ensures he keeps up with the work and also includes some activities outside the course, in particular relating to his planned family holiday in France.

As he is an early riser, he has planned short learning and revision activities first thing in the morning. The course and course materials are integrated into his plan as they include reading, listening, writing, grammar and vocabulary exercises and a link to a website where he can watch short videos and do interactive quizzes. His progress can be 'measured' by a number of short tests integrated into the course. He will be able to get speaking practice in class. At home, he sometimes reads short articles from French newspapers online and looks at French camping websites. He would like to try to find a tandem partner** to meet once a month after gaining some confidence from the course and getting into a good routine.

* See the Common European Framework of Reference (CEFR) levels: https://rm.coe.int/cefr-companion-volume-with-new-descriptors-2018/1680787989

** A tandem partner is someone whose mother tongue is your target language and who wants to learn your native or first language. Working with a tandem partner offers you an ideal opportunity to practise using the language in real communication. See Tip 16 *Learn with a tandem partner*.

The grey slots show essential activities, never to be missed, even if life becomes hectic! The time allocated to homework in such times can be reduced if necessary.

	Mon	Tues	Wed	Thurs	Fri	Sat	Sun
Morning	7 am 10 mins Vocabulary exercise or revision	7 am 10 mins Vocabulary exercise or revision	7 am 10 mins Vocabulary exercise or revision	7 am 10 mins Vocabulary exercise or revision	7 am 10 mins Vocabulary exercise or revision		
Midday					12 noon 60 mins Do French homework		
Afternoon				2 pm 90 mins French course			
Evening			8 pm 15 mins Review last week's course				Surf the net in French

Sample plan 2

Learner profile	Target language	Starting level	Timeframe	Global aim
Manager	Russian	Rusty advanced	6 months 2–3 hours a week	To speak fluently with new Russian business partners and their families and write simple emails

This learner studied Russian and Management at university in England. She hasn't used her Russian for over a decade, but now has a new job involving regular travel to Russia. She needs to brush up her rather rusty Russian and would also like to take advantage of cultural activities when in Russia.

Her job is time-consuming, but she can use some of her time travelling to and from work and when abroad to work on the language. As she is an experienced language learner, she has decided to study independently and use digital resources as much as possible. She will have a monthly private lesson with a teacher when she's in Russia for feedback and guidance on grammar points and emails. When very busy, she can simply cut back on some of the activities. But even 15 minutes a day on the train will pay off.

	Aims	Activities	Days/times/place	Measuring progress
Listening	Understand detail in natural spoken Russian, particularly on business topics and in meetings	Listen to podcasts and audio books on management Listen to short news summaries	On the train to work once or twice a week	Guess percentage understood. Listen to the same recordings again a few weeks/months later and reassess the percentage understood
Reading	Reinforce vocabulary and improve reading skills	Read an article from a Russian business journal or newspaper Read a novel	On the train to work once or twice a week On longer trips or in bed	Highlight and look up difficult words. Keep the texts and read them again in a few weeks
Vocabulary	Brush up forgotten words and learn some new ones, particularly job-related	Note and memorise useful words and phrases when listening or reading – try to use them when speaking	When reading/ listening and doing 5-minute memory practice once a day on weekdays	Test self. Do mind maps to see how many words I can remember
Speaking	Become more fluent and participate actively in meetings	Use every opportunity to speak to Russian colleagues including online and with the teacher	Weekly and when in Russia	See how much easier it becomes!
Grammar	Improve specific grammar points and eliminate habitual errors	Work with a grammar book based on the teacher's advice	Once a month, after having the teacher's feedback in the lesson	Work on a limited number of exercises of increasing difficulty
Writing	Write emails	Use online tutorials	Review emails sent to colleagues with the teacher	Review ease of writing and the teacher's feedback

Sample plan 3

Learner profile	Target language	Starting level	Timeframe	Global aim
Retirees	Survival Chinese	Beginner	1 year initially 6 or more hours a week	To be able to use and understand basic language on future holidays in China

These learners are a couple who have recently retired. They have been interested in China and Chinese culture for a long time and, after having an organised group holiday there recently, decided they wanted to learn some basics of the language and then travel more independently in the country. They have a lot of time, are highly motivated and think learning Chinese would be a good retirement project. Their mother tongue is English and they both speak a little French. They realise Chinese is a challenging language for westerners and have therefore set quite modest aims. They both play a musical instrument and hope that this will help in learning a tone language.

As they want to save their money for visiting China, they don't want to spend a lot on learning the language and they also don't want to attend regular classes. So their plan is intended to be cost effective and involves four basic approaches and some experimentation.

Aims		
To learn and practise using useful vocabulary and phrases for travelling in China To be able to make very basic conversation with Chinese people To understand some basic spoken Chinese To learn about Chinese customs and culture		
Learning sources, materials and activities	**Days/times**	**Measuring progress**
BBC online Chinese courses and BBC links to sources in China http://www.bbc.co.uk/languages/chinese/	2 hours, 3 mornings a week, for 1 year initially	Quizzes and tests on the website
Book written by Chinese specialists: *Easy Peasy CHINESE Mandarin for beginners* by Elinor Greenwood, Dorling Kindersley Ltd	To dip into from time to time	
Chinese university student tandem partner or partners – meet and speak English and very basic Chinese, practising what we have learnt independently	Once a month	See how much we can manage to say and understand each time
Local Confucius Institute to meet Chinese people and learn more about Chinese culture	Occasional events	

Over to you

Your individual learning plan

Now draw up a plan of your own. It doesn't need to be in a grid. It could be a short text or any format you find helpful. But it should be available for you to refer to regularly, to keep yourself on track.

When you have finished your plan, check that it corresponds to the criteria given for good language plans as outlined in Tip 6 *Draw up a plan*.

Use your learning plan for at least two weeks and then decide if you need to adjust it. Maybe you have been too ambitious or perhaps you need to change activities? You will find more ideas for your learning plan in Tip 11 *Integrate learning into your everyday routine*.

....

....

....

....

....

....

....

....

....

....

....

....

8 Set small, achievable goals

Everyone knows what it's like to start the New Year with at least one ambitious resolution – to spend an hour at the gym every day, to lose 10 kg, to write a novel, never to eat chocolate again, to stop procrastinating or to start your own business – only to reach the end of January putting on weight because of all the chocolate you're eating, having decided it would be better to join the gym and start the novel or the business next year instead. The problem is the very human tendency to set ourselves huge goals without thinking through all the steps we need to take to reach them. There is no reason why we can't achieve our aims, but we are much more likely to do so if we approach them by setting out small, easily achievable goals. Then our success in losing that first half kilo in a week or writing the outline for our novel will motivate us to take the next small step and carry on.

So, when it comes to language learning, what sorts of small goals could you set yourself? You could opt to do a couple of pages of a coursebook or a certain number of exercises every week. Or you could think about the sorts of things that you want to do with the language and base your goals on those. For example, if you've just started learning Greek with a view to a holiday in Corfu, you could set goals like this:

- Find a hotel registration form in Greek and practise filling it in.
- Learn how to say ten basic phrases like *Please, Thank you, Good morning, Goodbye*, etc.
- Find a menu from a Greek restaurant online and decide what to order.
- Learn how to order a coffee and cake in a café and ask for the bill.
- Look at a map of the place you're going to stay in and practise asking the way to different locations.

(See Section C for ideas on useful basic language.)

If you're a more advanced student studying Japanese in order to do business in Japan, then your goals could be:

- Do some research online to find out what you can about business etiquette in Japan and make notes of all the useful points you come across.
- Write notes describing what your company does and what your role is. Then practise explaining this to a Japanese acquaintance.
- Discuss with a Japanese colleague what sorts of things it would be useful to make small talk about and prepare some things you might be able to say in a situation where small talk is required. (See Tip 87 *Small talk / social talk*.)

- Listen to a recording of the news in Japanese and note down some useful vocabulary.
- Do six exercises in your coursebook relating to the language of business in Japanese.
- Look at the website of a major Japanese company and make notes of any phrases that interest you.

Whatever small, easily achievable short-term goals you set yourself, build in some breathing spaces. These will give you the opportunity to catch up if by any chance you have fallen a little behind, and if you haven't, then you will be able to use the break for some useful revision.

Reward yourself for achieving milestones

To help motivate yourself to make further progress, include in your plan little rewards for yourself as you achieve your goals. If possible, you could try making the rewards fit the task. So the Greek student could have a piece of baklava as a reward for mastering a menu in Greek. The Japanese student could visit a sushi bar where the staff are Japanese and, in addition to enjoying the sushi, practise some of the small talk he or she has been rehearsing at home.

Over to you

Make a list of some of the small, easily achievable goals that you think could help you have a productive language learning experience.

....

....

....

....

....

Note down some ideas for rewards that you could give yourself.

....

....

....

....

....

9 How do people learn foreign languages?

Despite much research into how people learn foreign languages, there are, as yet, no clear simple answers and no quick fixes. Some experts believe human beings are innately programmed to learn languages and that learning a foreign language may be easier when we are young. Others see language learning as similar to learning a skill where we build up knowledge of different elements or components of the language and improve or perfect that knowledge with practice.

One point to bear in mind is that language learning is not linear. However systematically you work, there will inevitably be frustrating plateaux, when you seem to be stuck and make no progress, followed by sudden, unexpected breakthroughs.

Here are some of the factors that are likely to have an impact on your ability to learn a language. Put a cross next to each point:

	Yes	No
Individual differences		
I'm extrovert / communicative.		
I don't worry about mistakes.		
I'm concerned about speaking correctly.		
I like analysing / doing exercises.		
I like learning by doing.		
I like having a teacher.		
I plan and reflect on learning.		
I like variety rather than routine in learning activities.		
Contextual factors		
Availability of technology		
Ease of access to teachers / tandem partners*		
Ease of contact with native speakers or advanced speakers		
	+ High	Low –
Level of motivation		
Need for target language		

* A tandem partner is someone whose mother tongue is your target language and who wants to learn your native or first language. Working with a tandem partner offers you an ideal opportunity to practise using the language in real communication. See Tip 16 *Learn with a tandem partner.*

Individual differences in the way people learn play a role. Some people are more adventurous than others, which can help as they are prepared to take risks and try speaking the language in challenging situations. Others are more analytical and like to understand the grammar before taking risks.

Ideally, it's good to find a balance between using the language spontaneously and understanding the rules. If you naturally 'pick up' language in ready-made phrases, you may seem to make a lot of progress initially, but unless you have some knowledge of the underlying system, you won't be able to generate a range of new language and may risk not getting beyond 'phrasebook' language. So being aware of the way you learn and experimenting with different approaches will help.

Technology can make your life easier, but people manage to learn languages in almost any circumstances because the overriding factors affecting language learning still tend to be motivation and needs. You may find language learning intrinsically motivating, in which case it can be a lifelong hobby, or you may need to pass an exam to be able to work in your field when you move to another country or change jobs. This can really push you to learn!

Over to you

What does the chart tell you about yourself, your attitude and approach to learning languages?

....

....

....

....

....

You'll have an opportunity to reflect more on this in the next tip.

10 What is a good language learner?

Studies carried out in the late 20th and early 21st centuries show that effective language learners tend to share a number of characteristics.

Of course, it's important to define 'effective', which can be done in relation to the learner's aims. If a learner wants to be able to function as a tourist with a basic knowledge of the language and learns enough language to do this, he or she can be said to have learnt effectively, without studying the whole grammatical system, having an extensive vocabulary or being able to read complex texts, for example. If, on the other hand, you want to train to teach your target language, you will have to devote more time to reach a higher level and not only be able to use the language at an advanced level, but also understand its grammar in much more detail than most users.

Good language learners:

1 are often highly motivated, either because they are passionate about the language or have a specific need such as getting married and moving to another country

2 plan and reflect on their learning

3 like to communicate, so they use all opportunities to practise using the language

4 don't worry too much about mistakes when communicating, but do spend time on understanding and practising the grammar relevant to their level

5 use a variety of language learning strategies.

Over to you

In what ways are you or do you have the potential to become a good language learner?

. . . .

. . . .

. . . .

. . . .

. . . .

. . . .

List your strengths in terms of language learning:

....

....

....

....

....

What two points could you improve?

....

....

....

....

....

Is there anything you want to think about more or experiment with?

....

....

....

....

....

Key points

In this section, we have considered making plans. Here are some key points to remember:

- Make sure you have a clear reason for learning a foreign language.
- Decide carefully which language to study.
- Plan your learning, beginning with a short written global aim.
- Break down the global aim into a series of micro-aims based on what you want to be able to do in the language.
- Identify learning activities that suit you so you can work towards your micro-aims.
- Draw up a learning schedule with regular learning slots and activities that fit in with your lifestyle.
- Fit rewards into your plan that you can enjoy when you achieve your goals.

My own take-home notes on Making plans

B Ways of learning

Learning is not attained by chance; it must be sought for with ardour and diligence.

Abigail Adams (1744–1818)

Throughout the ages, people have learnt languages in many different ways. Traders in the Middle Ages focused on the spoken language, negotiating shipments of spices, precious metals, silks and many other goods. At the same time, scholars were studying and translating ancient texts with a more academic approach. There are, indeed, many ways to learn a language and this section sets out to explore some of these in order to help you find the best approach or combination of approaches for you to maximise your progress and pleasure.

Language learning and teaching have tended to be subject to fashion, with new ways of learning being invented and reinvented and, more recently, often heavily marketed. As with many fashion fads, not all approaches to language learning survive in the long term, but scientific research has led to a more grounded way of viewing language learning and teaching, even if we still haven't figured out all the secrets of how people learn languages.

Aims of this section

In this section, we explore a range of ways of learning foreign languages, including the importance of adopting a systematic approach and integrating language learning into your life. We consider the many ways a language can be learnt, from taking a traditional language course to drawing on multiple digital resources. We are lucky to live in an age of digitalisation and the world wide web, with access to languages from all around the world and opportunities for language learning that were formerly unheard of.

It's often a good idea to combine different approaches to learning. For example, you could study in a class and also with a learning community or a tandem partner, while also using multiple online resources. In this way, you can benefit from variety and increase your opportunities to practise the language. This will help you maintain your motivation and thus your progress over the long term. We explain these approaches in the tips in this section.

The tips in this section show you:

- how to build regular language learning activities into your everyday life
- how to decide whether taking a language course locally or abroad is the best approach for you
- how to decide whether learning with a private teacher would suit you
- what the advantages can be of joining a learning community
- what a tandem partner is and how to decide whether you would benefit from learning with one
- ways of learning by doing, such as learning a skill or doing a hobby in the target language
- how to develop your language skills using online resources such as courses, apps and dictionaries
- how to learn with traditional resources online, such as newspapers and films
- how to use electronic versions of traditional resources such as newspapers, films and also e-books with integrated dictionaries
- how to use interactive online resources, such as social media, gaming apps and websites.

11 Integrate learning into your everyday routine

Language learning is sometimes compared to getting and staying fit. The more regularly you work on it, the better the results. In fact, one of the key factors in successful language learning is finding ways to integrate language learning activities into your daily and weekly routine. Little and often works well when learning a language so that you maintain your motivation and begin to see progress fairly quickly.

Work out when you have or can make time slots that you can use for language learning. These can be as short as five minutes, as long as 90 minutes, or somewhere in between. But beware of spending a long time doing lots of arduous exercises. As with fitness, you can overdo it and might find you're putting yourself off!

First thing in the morning and last thing at night can be good times to fit in short fulfilling activities. Here are some examples of five-minute exercises that work well for consolidating or revising grammar or vocabulary:

- work on a vocabulary training app
- do a short grammar exercise.

Other short activities could include:

- listen to a news summary
- read a short news report on a 'hot' story
- dip into a virtual museum tour
- listen to a song on YouTube while looking at the lyrics
- read a couple of pages from a novel.

You may be able to do some activities that take a little longer, say 20–30 minutes, when cooking, driving or doing sports such as jogging. Suitable sources could include:

- audio books / podcasts
- current affairs, the news or sports programmes on the radio.

Whatever you choose, it's important to find a topic that will really hold your attention.

Plan to budget time each week for a longer activity to gain extended exposure to the target language:

- watch a film – with or without subtitles – at home or in the cinema
- read a chapter from a book (using an online dictionary to save time)
- watch a television documentary.

What's most important though is developing a routine, so you work on the language in some way, if not every day, at least a few times each week and do your best not to slip out of the routine completely. A lot of progress can be made by taking regular small steps.

Over to you

Review the personal learning plan you drew up after reading Tip 7 *Learning plans in practice* in Section A and consider the ways different people fitted language learning into their weekly schedule. Now see if you can make adjustments to your plan based on the ideas above, inserting the kind of activities you could work on at different times during the week. You may need to experiment to find activities that are helpful and fun.

12 Sign up for a course locally

Advantages of taking a course

If you like learning in a group with other people, then a language learning class is an obvious choice. A class can be a suitable choice for language learners at any level.

Classroom learning means you will usually have a coursebook and often a workbook in addition to access to online materials. You may also have a grammar book. Modern learning materials are often lively and interesting and help you to learn useful language from the start. One of the advantages of having a book is that it gives you structure; you can see what you're going to be learning and look back to see how much progress you've made. Working with your classmates is often fun and stimulating.

Finding the 'right' course

You can find information on local language courses online, in public libraries and in adult education colleges. In many countries, there are approval schemes that validate the quality of teaching. In general, paying a lot for a course doesn't guarantee better training; in many places, public institutions run classes during the day and in the evenings that are relatively inexpensive and good quality. Some schools or colleges will allow you to sit in on a trial lesson before you decide to join.

A reputable language school will organise tests to make sure you're in a class that suits your level. There should be a pleasant and encouraging atmosphere in class and qualified teachers who will ensure that lessons are well planned and have clear aims. The teacher should be able to answer your questions and you should feel that you have learnt something in each lesson and are making progress over a period of weeks and months.

Getting the most from a course

To benefit from taking a course, attend classes regularly and do the homework! Before each class, review the previous lesson, checking key points. In class, don't sit next to the same person in each lesson. People have different learning styles and strengths and weaknesses. By changing partners regularly, you can complement each other in different ways.

If you feel you're getting left behind or there are things you don't understand, ask the teacher for advice and extra help. You may, on the other hand, find the course too easy. The teacher can perhaps offer additional exercises for you or arrange for you to be transferred to another class. People often worry that they will learn mistakes from other students in the class. On the whole, this isn't a problem as everyone progresses together and learners often help each other or ask the teacher if they are unsure if something is correct or not. The teacher will also give regular feedback to iron out problems.

Over to you

If you have decided you would like to sign up for a language class locally, then:

Look into all the options

How many hours of tuition do students have per week? ....

What is the timetable? ....

How much does the course cost? ....

What are the teachers' experience and qualifications?

....

How big are the classes? ....

Are you allowed to attend a free trial lesson? ....

Can you find out any information about past students' experiences, for example online?

....

Next steps

1 Decide which course to take. If you're unsure about anything, contact the school/college directly for advice.

2 Sign up!

3 Note in your diary exactly where the building and the classroom are and when you have to be there. It's not a good idea to be late for the first lesson or test!

I'm going to go to a language class at: ....

It starts on: ....

Before the class/course starts, I need to: ....

13 Consider taking a course abroad

If you have the time, resources and inclination, you could take a language course in a country where your target language is spoken, either for a few weeks or for a longer period as part of a gap year or sabbatical. This can be fun and can help you to make more rapid progress than with weekly courses.

Research different options carefully and also consider the time of year. In the summer, you might find yourself in a class with teenagers from the same country tending to speak their mother tongue together and showing more interest in partying than learning the language. This may or may not be a good experience!

For courses abroad, national organisations such as the Goethe-Institut in Germany or the Società Dante Alighieri in Italy specialise in foreign language courses. If you're following a course at home, your teacher will probably be able to give you guidance concerning such organisations. There is, of course, a plethora of information online. You can search for 'French as a foreign language courses in France', for example. However, one of the best ways to choose a school is through word of mouth. See if you can find someone who has done a course abroad and get their feedback.

Specialised courses

In some countries you can take specialised courses, for example learning the language in the morning and then going on cultural tours in the afternoon, or combining language learning with sport. Universities often provide courses for future students. These can be excellent if your level is already high.

Some courses are aimed at specific age groups – teenagers, young adults or the over-60s, for example. These may appeal but you can also gain from the variety of experience in a group with people of widely varying ages.

If you're learning a language for work, your company or organisation may be paying. In this case, they may provide names of suitable schools. Some companies work with schools that provide training specifically for professionals and business executives. Such courses offer very targeted learning and prepare you specifically for the workplace tasks you need to do in the language.

Some schools abroad may have representatives in your country to advise you on the courses and help you with arrangements for travel and accommodation. Of course, their job is also to 'sell' the courses.

Some schools abroad may also offer courses online that you can take without leaving home.

Over to you

If you have decided you would like to sign up for a language class abroad then, in addition to researching the points mentioned for local courses in Tip 12 *Sign up for a course locally*, you should also find answers to the following questions:

What kind of accommodation is offered?

....

....

How far is the accommodation from the school? ....

Is there good public transport from the accommodation to the school?

....

Is there a good mix of nationalities in the classes? ....

....

....

....

What is the average age of students in the classes? ....

Does the school organise social/cultural activities?

....

....

....

What are the payment/contractual arrangements?

....

....

....

14 Take private lessons

What about hiring a private teacher?

Taking private lessons either at home or abroad may suit you better than a course. You can take private lessons either face to face or with a virtual teacher using one of the many online platforms available. If you want to find a private teacher abroad, you may even live with a qualified teacher in his or her home in a country where your target language is spoken.

Many people, from students to retired teachers, give private lessons. You can find a teacher offering private courses on the noticeboard of a local college or through small ads or social media. You could also advertise for a teacher yourself. Prices for private lessons vary considerably. Expensive tuition doesn't necessarily mean better. Retired teachers, with a lifetime of experience, often offer reasonable rates.

Once you have found a teacher, discuss your needs. The teacher should be able to help you to set aims, and give you a clear idea of what can be achieved and how much work will be involved. You, in turn, should find out how much experience the teacher has had and what their teaching qualifications and background are. You may find it useful to arrange to have a few lessons initially, to see how you get on together.

If you're going to live with a teacher abroad, it will probably be wise to go through an official organisation that specialises in such courses.

Over to you

I would like to study with a private teacher because:

....

....

What do I expect from the teacher?

....

....

How can I find a suitable teacher?

....

....

15 Join a learning community

You may find it helpful to join a 'learning community'. This is a group of people who have similar aims and work together supporting each other. You can form your own learning community with classmates or even join a virtual learning community. These often have forums where you can share your experiences and find language learning resources and tips.

Learners who aren't working full time or who have an evening free can meet to work on the class homework together, practise speaking if their level is more advanced, or go to a film in the target language together from time to time.

Learning communities can also be informal groups of people sharing an interest in a language. Some groups are organised around reading and discussing a book or a film and may include native and non-native speakers, so they are suitable for more advanced learners. A group can also seek out opportunities in libraries, bookshops, cinemas and universities, particularly in big cities, where they can attend special events such as book readings.

One of the advantages of such groups is that regular attendance isn't usually essential. All of these variants on learning communities are, of course, very motivating and can lead to friendship and social contact that goes beyond learning the language. Learning communities certainly provide motivation, which is all-important in language learning, and virtual learning communities can be an option for those with less time or availability to meet face to face.

A learning community

Over to you

Do you like the idea of joining a learning community? ....

What kind of community would you consider joining – real or virtual?

....

How would being a member of a learning community suit:

- your lifestyle?

  ....

  ....

- the way you like to learn?

  ....

  ....

Bearing these points in mind, how would you go about finding or setting up a community?

....

....

....

....

....

....

16 Learn with a tandem partner

What is a tandem partner?

A tandem partner, also sometimes called a learning buddy, is someone whose native language is the language you want to learn. He or she wants to learn your native language. So learning a language with a tandem partner basically involves conversation exchange and practice, although you can also work on other skills such as reading with your partner.

Finding a tandem partner

Finding a tandem partner shouldn't be too difficult, although that will depend to some extent on which language you want to learn. You can work with a tandem partner either face to face or virtually using one of the many online platforms available. You can also download apps to find and work with tandem partners. If you live somewhere quite remote, you might need to have a virtual tandem partner. Universities and some schools often match potential partners up and, of course, it's possible to find someone via the internet.

Some basic principles

Your tandem partner may be much older or younger than you and may come from a very different background. However, what is important is that you're both willing to invest time in helping each other to learn your respective languages. You don't need to be at an equivalent level in terms of your knowledge of your target languages but language learners at beginner level aren't really suitable as tandem partners.

You need to decide together how much time you will spend working on the languages and how often to meet. For example, you could meet once a week or once a month. And you need to make sure you have sufficient time when you meet. At least an hour is necessary as you will need to spend 30 minutes speaking one language together and then switch language for a further 30 minutes. If you don't have much time, then you can do your tandem exchange over lunch or even going for a walk together so that you combine language learning and practice with activities you would be doing anyway.

A word of caution

In the beginning, always meet your partner in a public place. At the first meeting, it's important to get to know each other, discuss past learning experiences, how you like to learn and your current aims. You can draw up a work plan and schedule for regular meetings. Remember to be respectful concerning cultural differences and if you don't feel comfortable with your partner, you don't need to continue to meet.

What are the advantages of working with a tandem partner?

Working with a tandem partner can offer you a wonderful opportunity to really use the language without paying anything! As your tandem partner will be from a different culture to yours, you can also learn about their culture. Working with a tandem partner can be very effective in professional or academic contexts, but it can also lead to friendship, particularly when partners share hobbies or have common interests. For a partnership to work to its full potential, you both need to be able to speak reasonably fluently.

We discuss how to get the most out of working with a tandem partner in Tip 65 *Working with a tandem partner*.

Over to you

If I work with a tandem partner I would like to improve my:

....

....

....

The advantages for me would be:

....

....

....

In return, I could offer:

....

....

....

I would prefer to work with a tandem partner face to face / online because:

....

....

17 Learn by doing

When you learn a language by doing a non-language-related activity, you use the language for real communication rather than as a language learner. This means that you have to make yourself understood and understand those you're with, so you get a lot of opportunities to listen and expand your vocabulary. Depending on your aims, you may need to combine this form of learning with formal tuition.

Here are some of the kinds of activities that allow you to learn a language 'by doing'.

Studying in a foreign language

Student exchanges on offer are wide and varied these days. There are exchange programmes organised between universities and vocational organisations all over the world. Such programmes are challenging, but you will be able to put the language and experience on your CV/résumé, which will increase your potential when you begin your career.

Working in a foreign language

The level of language you need to do your job will depend on the job and context. Your company may send you abroad, or you may actively seek a post where you can use one or more foreign languages. If you're not yet in full-time employment, a holiday job such as grape picking, working with children on a summer camp or as a sports instructor can also offer a great opportunity to practise your target language. Whatever your starting level, you will certainly make progress as you have to make yourself understood and do your job.

Hobbies and non-language courses in a foreign language

This is an easy option if you live in a country where your target language is spoken. It can be a good backup for people working in the language and needing to improve their level without too much effort. Joining a choir or a golf club could be suitable options as they involve not only the activity itself, but often some social or relaxation time, which inevitably involves talking and getting to know people and the local culture.

If you don't live in a country where the target language is spoken, you could combine doing a practical non-language course such as cookery or a sport in your target language with a holiday in a country where the language is spoken. You should choose a course that allows opportunities to speak and possibly also includes social activities. You also have to be really interested in the topic of the course or skill you will be learning, so you can simply enjoy yourself; the learning will happen on its own.

Another possibility, if you aren't living in a country where your target language is spoken, is to find online videos in your target language explaining how to do things that you want to learn. If you're studying French you could, for example, find an online video of someone demonstrating a recipe in French or explaining how to do some craft or another activity that interests you.

Doing voluntary work

If you're living or staying in a country where the target language is spoken, doing voluntary work can be a win-win opportunity, if you have time. Choose work that involves a lot of interaction with other people who are either native speakers or whose language skills are very advanced. For example, you could help with a meal delivery service that involves travelling around with a driver and taking meals to the elderly. You will have many opportunities to talk to both the driver and the 'customers'.

Over to you

If learning by doing appeals to you, what activities could you get involved in?

....

....

....

Consider which of the activities you noted above appeals to you most and list the different opportunities open to you to learn by doing:

....

....

....

Where can you find out about these opportunities?

....

....

....

18 Research online learning resources

The internet has revolutionised language learning. With a mobile phone or tablet, we can now access a wide range of resources for language learning from all around the world.

Here are some of the ways you can develop your language skills using online resources.

Online courses

If you can't join a regular language course and you're happy to study independently, you might find an online course that fits your needs. There are many private and publicly funded courses and you don't always need to spend a lot of money for a good quality course.

Some countries have national Open Universities that offer general online language courses developed by experts and with individual support for learners. Some universities, such as Harvard, also offer excellent free online courses for a range of languages (see www.edx.org). Public broadcasting companies, such as the BBC in the UK or Deutsche Welle in Germany, offer excellent free language training with lots of interactive learning activities.

One note of caution though, do beware of heavily marketed language courses that promise ultra-swift results – language learning takes time!

Language learning apps

Some of the courses mentioned above are available in the form of apps, although these may not be available for all languages. For example, there are very helpful apps such as *Quizlet*, which is an open-source app that provides a variety of exercises to practise grammar and vocabulary. You can download a number of free exercises on this. These exercises are often developed by language teachers and can be particularly helpful in giving you bite-sized exercises that you can work on any time you have a free moment.

There are also many commercial apps for language learning, some of which are free, at least initially. Choose those recommended by other users and be prepared to be asked to sign up for fee-paying courses.

Dictionary apps

Most of the top-quality bilingual and monolingual dictionaries have online apps. Ask a teacher or specialist in a bookshop to recommend the best dictionaries for your target language. You can then download the most appropriate dictionary app for your needs, either for a fee or free. If you choose the free version, the only disadvantage will be the advertisements, but you can ignore those. Having a dictionary app is a definite must for any language learner who likes to use technology.

Over to you

Explore public service TV and radio language courses offered in your target language.

Make notes on specific channels and programmes that you can begin to listen to or watch. You may be able to record TV programmes or download radio podcasts.

....

....

....

....

Download *Quizlet* and practise a vocabulary learning exercise in your target language. What type of exercise are you going to start with?

....

....

Do some research on quality dictionaries and see what bilingual dictionary apps are available free. Make notes on the ones you like the look of. Download one and start using it.

....

....

....

....

19 Access traditional resources online

Here we review traditional resources for language learning that you can access online. Later in the book we explore how these resources can be used most effectively in language learning. See Sections D, E and F.

Newspapers and magazines

For your chosen language, you will almost certainly be able to read newspapers online, or even download apps for the papers. You may need to do some research online to determine the quality of the newspaper you choose, or you might like to read a range of newspapers.

If you're just beginning to learn a language, you could consider reading free daily newspapers distributed in many countries for commuters. They are intended to be read on the train going to work and tend to have short articles, which are ideal to read when learning a language. You can access them online as apps or on your laptop or tablet and you may decide to read a short article once or twice a week, or even every day.

Most magazines also have a lot of interesting free material online. The same magazine, for example *Elle*, often has multiple language editions. The advantage of reading a magazine online is not only that it's often free, but also that you can choose a magazine relating to your hobby or special interest, which will be all the more motivating.

Streamed films / video on demand / cable TV

If you're fortunate enough to have access to streamed films, video on demand or cable TV, you can really take advantage of the enormous range offered in your target language. You may be able to borrow DVDs from your library and a lot of films are available online, for example on YouTube. Films and video are often available with subtitles and all of these media can be viewed several times. You may also be able to subscribe to platforms such as Netflix or Amazon Prime for even more choice.

Electronic books with integrated dictionaries

If you like reading, electronic books (e-books) are available commercially or through public libraries in some places. With an electronic reader, or your tablet or phone, you can download books in your target language. This means you always have a book at hand and can easily read a few pages or chapters at any time. *Project*

Gutenberg is an online community project that provides free electronic versions of thousands of books in many languages. The site is well worth visiting for any language learner: https://www.gutenberg.org/

Some electronic readers have dictionaries already installed when you buy them. If not, installing a digital bilingual dictionary will be helpful and time-saving.

Over to you

Try to do at least two of the following activities. Make a note of your plans below.

Find a newspaper in your target language that suits your level and read one short article. Use an online dictionary if necessary.

....

....

....

....

Find and watch a film in your target language with or without subtitles. It could be a film you have already seen and enjoyed in your own language.

....

....

....

....

Download a book in your target language to your tablet, phone or electronic reader. You may be able to experiment with an e-reader in your local library or a bookshop. Do some reading in this way and see if this kind of activity suits you.

....

....

....

....

20 Research interactive online resources

Social media

If you use social media in your own language, this could be an ideal language learning tool for you. Here we look at social media resources for language learning.

These are some of the ways and means social media can be used for language learning:

Social networking – sites such as Facebook and LinkedIn offer opportunities not just to read and watch interesting material but also to take part in interactive discussions.

Online forums – if you have a special interest, you may already be used to accessing or contributing to online forums. Try accessing some in your target language.

Blogs and vlogs – reading blogs and watching vlogs can be a great way to improve your reading and listening skills while extending your vocabulary. If you want to improve your writing, you could begin writing your own blog; this could be a good activity to do with your teacher or tandem partner, if they help you edit the blog before you publish it.

Gaming apps

If you like online gaming, take advantage of gaming communities around the world to practise your target language. Most MMOs (massively multiplayer online) games are not intended specifically for language learners, but they are often international. Once you reach intermediate level in the language you're learning, you can take advantage of chat functions to interact with players from around the world in your target language. Using the language in this way for real communication, even if it isn't face to face, will help you to make progress and maintain motivation. Video games, in particular, provide extra contextual information that makes understanding and learning easier.

YouTube

YouTube videos can be filtered for content, length and access to transcripts. Although not intended for language learning, YouTube is a wonderful language learning tool. It's particularly effective in helping to improve listening skills and vocabulary.

Websites

Even when websites are not intended for language learning, they offer a wealth of stimulating material for reading and listening, and sometimes interactive activities such as questionnaires or quizzes.

Over to you

What types of electronic resources do you use in your own language?

....

How could you explore the possibilities for using them in your target language?

....

Here are just a few websites that you may already know. They are available in different languages: Lonely Planet, National Geographic, Wikipedia.

Surf the internet to improve your target language reading and listening skills. Find a website and then a topic that interests you and begin reading or listening.

....

....

....

You might also like to look at company websites, for example Zara for fashion (https://www.zara.com/es/) or Atletico Madrid (https://www.atleticodemadrid.com/) for football if Spanish is your target language.

What other websites can you find in your target language that you would like to explore? Make a note of them below. If you go to Google Translate and insert a website address, you can get a translation of that website into the language of your choice.

....

....

....

....

....

Key points

In this section, we have considered ways of learning. Here are some key points to remember:

- Plan regular times and activities during the week to focus on language learning.
- Look into taking a language course locally or perhaps even abroad.
- Consider private lessons if a language class doesn't suit your needs.
- Join a learning community or find a tandem partner for extra practice.
- Find ways to learn by doing, for example linked with a hobby such as cooking.
- Research online opportunities for learning and practice.

My own take-home notes on Ways of learning

C Focusing on things you're (almost) sure to need

A new language is a new life.

Persian proverb

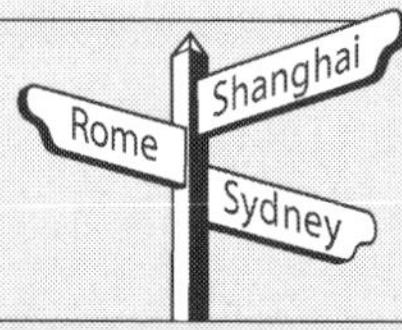

This section is rather different from other sections in the book. It involves you making a collection of useful words and phrases in your target language. Being comfortable with the words and expressions we're suggesting you collect will help you make friendly contact with others and do at least some of the things you want to do without falling back on your native language.

Over the next few pages you will be creating your own personal collection of useful phrases. In fact, much of each tip resembles an Over to you activity.

Published phrasebooks of the past have been known to cover a wide range of scenarios. Some examples from past phrasebooks are:

'The postillion has been struck by lightning.'

'Tell me, is left-handedness a common phenomenon in Transcaucasia?'

'Please direct me to a competent hypnotherapist.'

'I have brought 10 kg of rice for your family.'

'Keep your hands to yourself.'

Phrases like these are unlikely to be of much use to you.

Aims of this section

The tips in this section show you how to:

- collect some of the words and phrases that you're most likely to need when you're making your first forays into using the language
- focus on language that you yourself are likely to need, rather than phrases that may be out of date or of little practical use.

You could find out how to say the things we recommend you learn by turning to a good dictionary or by using one of these tools:

Google Translate https://translate.google.com

DeepL https://www.deepl.com/en/translator

However, if possible, use a native or other good speaker of your target language. Such a person will be able to help you with pronunciation. You should also take the opportunity to get them to share other information such as what sounds polite and when language is appropriate or inappropriate.

21 Survival phrases

Being polite and friendly

For most of us, the joy of learning a language lies in extending our ability to make contact with others. Simple phrases like those below show a willingness to communicate through the other person's language. They suggest that you're friendly and polite even if your knowledge of the language is still minimal.

Hello ....

Goodbye ....

Good morning ....

Good afternoon ....

Good evening ....

Good night ....

Please ....

Thank you ....

Excuse me ....

I don't understand ....

I only speak a little (Spanish) ....

I like it very much here ....

Basic travel needs

Visiting a place where your target language is spoken means that you immediately need to know certain words and phrases.

Exit ....

Entrance ....

Restaurant ....

Hotel ....

Bank ....

Garage / Petrol station ....

Car park ....

Open ....

Closed ....

Ladies ....

Gents ....

Where is the toilet, please? ....

....

What's the wi-fi password? ....

Can I have a coffee / beer / sandwich / the bill, please? ....

....

Can I have some ice cream / water / red wine, please? ....

....

How much does it cost? ....

(See Tip 29 *Are you ready to order?*)

Over to you

Do you think all the words and phrases on these pages would be useful for you? Which do you already know in your target language? Write them down next to their translation.

Find out how to say any remaining expressions you're not sure of and write them down too. If possible, find out what the translations are by asking a native or other good speaker of the language rather than using a dictionary, as they may share extra useful information about when and how the expressions are used in practice.

Ask your informant to suggest other phrases that they feel you should learn. For example, in some countries it's important to say something like 'Bon appétit' before eating a meal.

....

....

....

....

....

22 My name is ...

Whether you're striking up a conversation on a train, signing into a hotel or making a new acquaintance at a conference, you will need basic language to talk about who you are. Look at the phrases below and alter them to make them about yourself.

Then find out how to say them in your target language.

My name is Felicity O'Dell.

....

I'm British ....

I was born in Scotland ....

I live in Cambridge ....

Cambridge is a town in the south of England.

....

I'm a teacher ....

I work in a language school ....

I'm married ....

I have one son ....

As well as these things, which everyone is likely to need, there will be some things which are more particular to you. For example, do any of these phrases apply to you? If so, find out how to say them in your target language.

I'm a vegetarian / vegan. ....

I don't eat pork. ....

I'm allergic to peanuts / shellfish / eggs. ....

I'm deaf in my right ear. ....

Over to you

Make a note of some other useful expressions that you know you often need when talking about yourself to someone new. Write them down with their translations.

....

....

....

....

....

....

....

....

....

....

....

23 As easy as A, B, C

You might think that you don't need to learn how speakers say the letters of the alphabet in your target language – if your target language uses an alphabet, of course – but it's a useful skill to have. Why? It allows you to both give and understand spellings. You're quite likely to be asked to spell your name, for example, when you're making a reservation or ordering something over the phone. Similarly, you will sometimes want to request a spelling – you might need to check an address or ask someone to spell an unfamiliar word you hear so you can look it up.

Even if the language you're learning uses the same letters as English, the way they are pronounced will be different. The letter 'i' in French, for example, is pronounced much as the letter 'e' is pronounced in English. So you need lots of practice in both saying and understanding the names of the letters.

It's also necessary to learn the order of the letters in your target language. Without that knowledge, it becomes a slow process to look up a word in a print dictionary or to find something in an alphabetised list. The Cyrillic alphabet initially has many similarities with the alphabet used by English – it begins with the sounds 'a' and 'b' – but the third letter is a 'v' sound rather than a 'c'.

So how can you set about learning the alphabet of your target language? Do a web search for, for example, 'German alphabet pronunciation' or 'Russian alphabet pronunciation' and you will be offered links to an audio version of the alphabet you need. It's worth learning by heart in the way small children do. There may even be a song or rhyme to help you do this.

How can you practise using the letters? The main things to practise are the things you're most likely to be asked to spell – your own name, address and email address in particular. So repeat those until it's second nature to you. Keep practising spelling out new words in your head as you note them down in a vocabulary notebook. See Tip 35 *Recording vocabulary* for more ideas about vocabulary notebooks. If possible, practise with a friend by spelling out words for each other to write down, so you get used to hearing the letters as well as using them yourself.

Playing Hangman with a friend can be an enjoyable way to practise naming letters. One person chooses a word and writes down a dash for each letter. They also draw a gallows. Their partner then guesses letters. If the letter is correct, it is written above the right dash or dashes. If it isn't correct, then part of a body is drawn on the gallows. The body has a head, a torso, two arms and two legs and sometimes hands and feet. The aim is to guess the word before the body is complete!

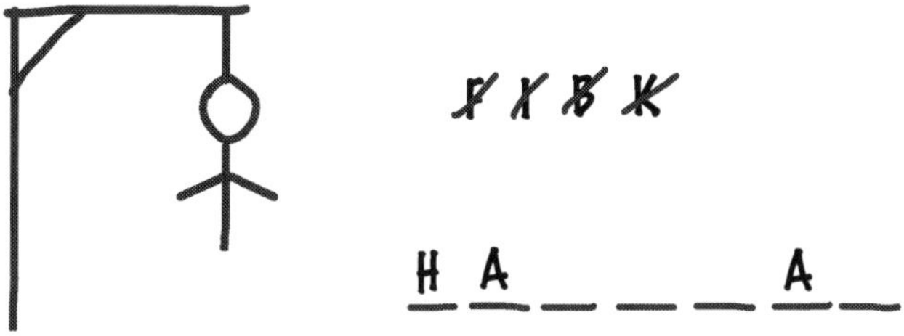

If you don't know the game of Hangman, you can find little videos showing how to play it on YouTube.

If your target language is one that isn't based on an alphabet – Chinese or Japanese words, for example, are written as characters or ideograms (symbols conveying the concept rather than the sound) – then your task will be slightly different. For Chinese, you will need to learn *pinyin*, the official system for describing Chinese words in terms of their pronunciation. Japanese has two sound-based writing systems – *katakana* and *hiragana* – for you to master.

Over to you

If your target language uses an alphabet, find out how to say the alphabet in it and practise saying it until you know it by heart. Which letters do you find most difficult? Find some words that use those letters and practise spelling them aloud.

....

....

....

....

If your target language isn't based on an alphabet system, ask a teacher or someone else who knows the language well to explain how you would spell your own name for someone who only speaks that language. Practise spelling both your name and address with them.

....

....

....

....

24 5, 4, 3, 2, 1, lift-off …

Numbers are one of the key things you need to learn – whether it's to know which hotel room is yours, to give a colleague your phone number or to understand how much something costs.

Write down how these numbers are said in your target language.

1	11	20	101 ....
2	12	21	200 ....
3	13	30	300 ....
4	14	40	400 ....
5	15	50	500 ....
6	16	60	1,000 ....
7	17	70	2,500 ....
8	18	80	5,000 ....
9	19	90	1,000,000 ....
10	20	100	2,000,000 ....

In English, the words for the numbers 13 to 19 as well as those for 20, 30, 40, 50, 60, 70, 80 and 90 are clearly linked to the single digit numbers they relate to. Do you see any similar patterns in your target language? If so, this should help you to remember the words.

In English, we usually refer to years as, for example, 'ten sixty-six' (1066) or 'twenty twenty' (2020). Does your target language do it in the same way or would it say, instead, 'one thousand and sixty-six' or 'two thousand and twenty'?

So, in what ways can you help yourself to learn and practise numbers? You could start by noting the numbers that are important to you.

Your apartment and/or house number ....

Your postcode / zip code ....

Your phone number(s) ....

Your car registration ....

Your passport / ID number ....

Your age ....

Your date of birth ....

Other important years for you ....

Your favourite number ....

Other important numbers for you ....

Over to you

If possible, make a recording of a native speaker or advanced speaker of your target language saying the numbers in this tip.

Practise speaking with the recording until you feel perfectly fluent with the numbers.

Practise more numbers by writing down sums for yourself, e.g. 423 + 765 = ? Then say the numbers aloud as you do the sum.

....

....

....

....

....

It's also essential to be able to understand numbers accurately. Try to find someone who will reel off a stream of prices or phone numbers for you to write down. Practise doing it at speed until you get to the point where you feel you're relating the words directly to the numbers rather than translating them first.

....

....

....

....

....

25 Diaries and calendars

You need to know the words for the days of the week and for months in order to arrange meetings, book hotel rooms and restaurants, understand which days are public holidays or market days, or when someone's birthday is. So write down the words for the days and months in your target language.

January	....	Monday	....
February	....	Tuesday	....
March	....	Wednesday	....
April	....	Thursday	....
May	....	Friday	....
June	....	Saturday	....
July	....	Sunday	....
August	....		
September	....		
October	....		
November	....		
December	....		

Do the words you have written bear any resemblance to their English equivalents or to those in any other language you're familiar with? If so, this will help you to remember them.

Write the answers to these questions:

What day of the week is it today? ....

What day will it be tomorrow? ....

What day was it yesterday? ....

Which day of the week were you born on? If you don't know, you can find this out at: http://www.springfrog.com/calculator/day-week.htm

....

What month is it now? ....

What month is your birthday? ....

In what months do your closest friends and family have birthdays?

....

....

Over to you

Remind yourself every day of the words in this tip by writing the appropriate day and month on a sticky note and putting it on your computer screen or on the mirror in the bathroom.

Next time you get a diary or calendar, try to get hold of one in your target language.

26 Keeping track of time

It's not enough just to be able to specify days and months. Sometimes you need to be more precise. You may, for example, need to be able to understand the suggestion *Let's meet at half past seven* or the answer to a question such as *What time does the train leave?*

Increasingly, with people telling the time more from mobile phones or fitness tracker displays rather than traditional watches, time is expressed digitally, e.g. *The film starts at seven fifteen* rather than *The film starts at quarter past seven*. It's still necessary, however, to understand both ways of telling the time even if you personally decide you're only going to do it one way or the other.

So, find out how to say the following times in your target language.

What's the time? / What time is it?

....

It's seven o'clock.  ....

It's ten past seven.  ....

It's quarter past seven. ....

It's seven fifteen. ....

It's half past seven. ....

It's seven thirty. ....

It's twenty to eight.  ....

It's quarter to eight. ....

It's seven forty-five. ....

Answer any of the following questions that are relevant for you, giving the time in your target language.

What time do you usually wake up? ....

What time do you usually get up? ....

What time do you have breakfast? ....

What time do you leave home? ....

What time do you start work? ....

What time do you have lunch? ....

What time do you stop work? ....

What time do you get home? ....

What time do you have dinner? ....

What time do you go to bed? ....

What time do you fall asleep? ....

What time do you usually get up at the weekend? ....

What time do you usually go to bed at the weekend? ....

Here are some other useful words and phrases for talking about time. Find out and make a note of their equivalents in your target language.

Last year ....

Last week ....

Yesterday ....

Tomorrow ....

Next week ....

Next year ....

Knowing these phrases will help you make your meaning clear even if you can't use verbs accurately. If you say *I go to Paris last year* or *We go to Australia next week*, the listener will understand what you mean despite the fact that you haven't been able to say *I went* or *We're going to go*. In fact, some languages – Chinese, for example – don't even require you to change the verb form, the use of the time phrase is quite enough.

Over to you

Does your target language express time in the same way as your first language? In English, for example, we say *half past two*, whereas in Russian the equivalent time translates literally as *half of the third*.

....

....

....

....

....

Each time you check the time during the day, practise in your head how you would say it in your target language.

27 Buying stuff

Travelling usually involves a bit of shopping, whether it's buying a charger because you left yours at home or getting a souvenir or a present for the neighbour who is feeding your cat. So what is the essential language for shopping?

Firstly, it can be useful to know the names of different types of shops. Find the words in your target language for the following places where you can buy things:

Chemist / Pharmacy ....

Bank / Post office ....

Market ....

Supermarket ....

Department store ....

Baker's ....

Bookshop ....

Newsagent ....

Different countries sometimes have rather different shopping traditions and it can be useful to check whether this is the case in advance of a visit. Try to find someone familiar with the culture you're planning to visit who can explain what the situation is there and how it contrasts with what you're accustomed to. Is it normal, for example, to haggle over prices? If so, how is this usually done? Is there any special language that would help you appear less like a tourist and more like someone who is aware of the local culture?

It's important to be able to ask this question:

How much does it cost? / How much is it? ....

Understanding the answer should be easy if you have followed the advice in Tip 24.

Some other useful questions are:

Where can I buy ...? ....

Where do I pay? ....

Can I pay by card / with my phone? ....

In a restaurant you will probably want to say:

Can I have the bill, please? ....

And if you're a business traveller, you may need to ask:

Can I have a receipt, please? ....

Over to you

If possible, practise using the questions in this tip with a good speaker of your target language. Imagine you're in a shop together and he or she is the shop assistant. After you've asked the question, he or she should give you a straightforward answer. Can you understand the reply? Gestures and the tone of language used should help even if the words are unfamiliar.

If you haven't got someone to do this with, then you can still practise on your own. When you shop for something in your own language, practise afterwards saying what you might have said to the sales assistant in your target language.

Make a list in your target language of things you're likely to buy if you go as a tourist to a place where that language is spoken – stamps, postcards, a T-shirt, for example.

....

....

....

....

....

....

....

....

....

....

28 Finding your way around

A map on paper or on your phone plus a little bit of basic language will help you find your way around a new place. Note down the words in your target language for the following:

Excuse me! Where is ... .

the city centre? ....

the train station? ....

platform 10? ....

the bus station? ....

the airport? ....

the museum? ....

the nearest bank / bus stop / underground station / post office?

....

It isn't enough to be able to ask the question, you also need to understand the answer. The following phrases will give you a good start:

Turn left / right ....

Go straight on ....

It's on the left / right ....

Finding your way around is likely to involve using transport and there is plenty of key language you can learn to prepare yourself for this:

I'd like a single ticket to ... .

I'd like a return ticket to ... .

Can I order a taxi to ..., please? ....

Where do I buy a ticket for the bus? ....

Using these phrases is a step beyond just learning individual words. So you will need to practise them to feel comfortable and confident when you have the opportunity to use them in a natural context. If possible, find a native speaker or someone who speaks the language well to record them for you. Then practise listening and repeating until you feel you're reproducing the recording as closely as possible. This, of course, is something you can usefully do with any examples of language that you would like to learn.

Over to you

If you're planning a visit to a country where your target language is spoken, look online for maps and information about transport in the area. What does that suggest about words and phrases that could be useful for you to know? In some places, for example, you might want to know the words for *underground station, football stadium* and *cathedral,* whereas elsewhere *zoo, royal palace, tram* and *beach* might be more useful.

Make a list of those places. Then write the questions that you could use to ask where some of these places are.

....

....

....

....

....

....

....

....

....

29 Are you ready to order?

Menu language is one of the most practical and useful things to learn before visiting a place where your target language is spoken. In fact, you may already know quite a few words for food and drink as languages often borrow words for foods and drinks straight from their country of origin. If you're planning to learn Italian, for example, you will almost certainly already know *pasta, pizza, lasagne, espresso* and *gelato*. Write down any words that you already know in your target language for things that you might see on a menu.

....

....

....

....

....

As you may already know the words for things to eat, try putting them in phrases so that you not only get what you want but also sound more natural and thus polite. Find out how to say:

I'd like ... .

Can I have ... ? ....

Have you got ...? ....

Now try completing these phrases with things that you think you're almost certain to want to say when you're in a café or restaurant. For example, *I'd like a large black coffee, please. Can I have some bread? Have you got sparkling water?*

....

....

....

....

....

....

....

Over to you

Look online for a restaurant in a city in the country where your target language is spoken. On its website you will probably be able to find an example of its menu. Look at it and decide what you would choose if you were going to eat a meal there. Write down any interesting words and expressions you learn from the menu.

....

....

....

....

....

....

....

....

....

....

30 Improving communication

In the last tip in this section, we look at expressions relating to language and communication. They are questions or requests that you will almost certainly need when you first use your target language. They will help you to have successful interactions and will allow you to extend your knowledge of the language at the same time. Find out how to say the following things in your target language. You can either ask a teacher or other good speaker of your target language to help you do this or you could find out by using an online translator such as Google Translate.

I'm sorry, I don't understand.

....

Can you say that again, please?

....

Can you speak more slowly, please?

....

Can you say that again in other words?

....

What does X mean?

....

And, if all else fails:

Do you speak English? ....

Over to you

If possible, record a native or other good speaker of your target language saying these phrases – on your phone, perhaps – and then practise saying each phrase along with the recording to mimic the way he or she speaks as closely as possible.

Now you have come to the end of this section, read through and revise all the words and phrases you have noted down.

Key points

In this section, we have considered some of the language you're (almost) sure to need whatever your target language may be. Here are some key points to remember:

- The words and phrases covered in this section will be useful regardless of whether you're planning to use your target language primarily for leisure, study or work purposes.
- The collection of words and phrases that you've made in this section is the sort of language you're most likely to use when travelling in an area where your target language is spoken.
- This personal collection will be much more useful for you than a traditional phrasebook in that it's focused on your own personal needs.
- Of course, you're bound to have a need for other unpredictable language too, but mastering the kind of language we have focused on here will pay dividends in increasing your confidence when it comes to using the language to communicate in real situations.

My own take-home notes on Focusing on things you're (almost) sure to need

....

....

....

....

....

....

....

....

....

....

....

....

....

D Learning words

Words are, of course, the most powerful drug used by mankind.
Rudyard Kipling (1865–1936)

People sometimes think that learning a language is all about grammar. But you can do very little with a language if you only know about its grammar. You need vocabulary or 'content words', i.e. words such as *child, happy* or *swim*, that stand for something meaningful, as opposed to 'grammar words' such as *the, for* or *which*, that are simply used to clarify the relationship between content words. Knowing content words but no grammar can get you a long way when you're learning a new language – although we are certainly not suggesting that you ignore grammar.

Aims of this section

In this section, we provide tips to help you master the vocabulary of your target language as effectively as possible.

The tips here show you:

- some of the terms that it's useful to know when talking about vocabulary
- what it means to know a word
- why a good dictionary is important and how to choose one
- how to use tools to help you learn vocabulary
- how to keep a vocabulary notebook and the importance of revising vocabulary
- how to decide which types of vocabulary are most useful for you
- how to build up your vocabulary with words you already know
- ways to connect words with concepts
- how to make connections between words
- ways to help you remember vocabulary by making it more personal
- ways of memorising words.

In our discussion of the different vocabulary tips and tricks we present in this section of the book, we provide examples from English. However, each tip concludes with an Over to you activity asking you to relate the points that have been made to your target language.

31 The vocabulary of vocabulary

Let's start with a look at some of the basic terminology relating to learning vocabulary. While we don't believe it's necessary to know a lot of specialist linguistics terminology when studying a language, there are certain key words for concepts that it's helpful to understand. These may or may not already be familiar to you. Let's try a little quiz to check what you know.

Can you match the word on the left to its meaning on the right?

Word	**Meaning**
noun	most basic part of a word to which other parts can be added
verb	word that goes before a noun to show how it's related to another word
adjective	word expressing doing or being
adverb	letter or group of letters added to the beginning of a word (a prefix) or its ending (a suffix) to make a new word
preposition	word describing how something is done or happens
idiom	word describing a person, place, thing or idea
root	word representing the name of a person, place, thing or idea
affix	expression with a meaning that is not immediately obvious from the meanings of the individual words in it

In the box below there are two examples for each of these concepts. Can you match them up?

> sell like hot cakes   press in *oppressive* and *impression*   quickly
> spell   preview   during   tooth   happy   translate
> happiness   on   suddenly   easy   help in *unhelpful* and *helpless*
> pronunciation   keep an eye on

You will find the answers on page 109.

Over to you

Can you add an example from both your own and your target language for each of the words listed? It may not be possible to do this for all languages – not all languages use prepositions, for example, preferring to express relationships between nouns in other ways, often by adding affixes.

noun ....

verb ....

adjective ....

adverb ....

preposition ....

idiom ....

root ....

affix ....

32 What does knowing a word mean?

Knowing what a word means is only part of what you need to know about a word. An example from English will serve to illustrate our point but the same general points are true of any language, even if some of the specific points mentioned assume greater importance in some languages than others.

Let's take the word *tooth*, for example. Learners of English may know what *tooth* means, but if they want to use it properly, they need to know that it has an irregular plural (*teeth*), that it rhymes with *truth* but not *smooth* and that it's often found in combination with certain other words – *to clean your teeth*, *false teeth* and *have toothache*, for example. If learners are more advanced they may also be interested in idiomatic expressions like *have a sweet tooth* and *fight tooth and nail* as well as expressions with particular cultural associations like the *tooth fairy*. They may also be interested in ways in which the basic meaning of *tooth* expands into metaphorical meanings such as the *teeth of a comb*. Branching off in different directions, they may find it useful at the same time to notice the adjective *toothless* and the associated verb *teethe* (used not only about babies but in the more generally useful phrase *teething problems*).

With some words it's also important to know about connotations. That is a term used to refer to any particular associations that a word has. For example, there are lots of synonyms in English for *thin*. However, they have different connotations. An English-speaking person who is thin might be pleased if you called them *slim* (as that word suggests that you like the way they look) but they would feel insulted if you referred to them as *scrawny* (as that word has connotations of ugliness). If you called them *emaciated*, they would know that you were worried about their health.

In other words, knowing a word means knowing about:

- meaning
- spelling
- pronunciation
- word grammar
- words frequently used in combination with it.

With some words, knowing the word may also involve knowing about:

- words based on the same root
- idioms using the word
- special cultural associations that the word may have
- connotations.

Over to you

Which of these aspects of knowing a word do you think might be particularly important when you're working on your target language? In some languages, word grammar, for example, is much more complex than in others. Similarly, some languages form lots of words from one basic root much more than others do.

....

....

....

....

....

....

Choose one of these words to research in your target language – *sun, tree, baker, lazy, to earn*. Note down all you can find out about its meaning, spelling, pronunciation, word grammar, words frequently used with it, words based on the same root, idioms and any special cultural associations or connotations.

....

....

....

....

....

....

....

....

....

33 Choosing a dictionary

Having the right tools at your disposal can help to simplify the task of vocabulary learning. The most important tool for a language learner is a good dictionary.

What makes a good dictionary? Ideally you don't want one that simply translates between your own language and your target language. While that may work for words that relate to one simple easily identifiable thing like, say, *robin* or *motorbike*, it isn't enough. As Marek Kohn puts it in his excellent book, *Four Words for Friend*, 'Words in different languages rarely occupy exactly the same space of meaning.' His title is based on the point that the English word *friend* can be translated into Russian in at least four different ways, each of which suggests a differing degree of closeness in the relationship. So it's worth searching for as reliable a translation dictionary as there is. If possible, ask a teacher for advice; alternatively, you may be able to find recommendations online. It's probable that the most suitable dictionary will turn out to be an app or online as those are easy to keep up to date as well as straightforward to use. There are, for example, very convenient dictionary apps that you can install on your phone. These then allow you simply to click on any word in a text that you want to look up. However, make sure that you choose a good app or online dictionary, preferably one produced by an established dictionary publisher.

Ideally, you may also be able to benefit from a dictionary that is monolingual in the target language but aimed at learners of that language, giving plenty of examples of words in use as well as simple explanations of meaning. This will promote your learning in a number of different ways. If you look up the meaning of an unfamiliar word, you will then be associating that word with its explanation in your target language rather than with its translation, and avoiding translation is generally considered to be a much sounder approach to language acquisition. In addition, there is the mere fact that by looking at the explanation you're giving yourself practice in comprehension of your target language. Finally, through its examples, such a dictionary will help you see how the word is actually used, which will help you to use it accurately in your own speech or writing.

So choosing a dictionary means asking yourself the following questions – though you won't need to research every word you look up as fully as these questions suggest, especially when you're just starting to learn your target language:

- Does this dictionary show me how to spell words (in their various forms if these are not regular)?
- Does it show me how to pronounce words? Does the dictionary have audio so I can hear the pronunciation of the word?

- Does it give relevant information about the grammar of words? This includes both information about irregular forms of such things as plurals or past tenses and also information about structures used with certain words – *depend on someone*, for example, or *advise someone to do something*, to give some examples from English.
- Does it give examples of words in use?
- Does it indicate which words are typically found in combination with the word being looked up?
- Does it give examples of words with the same root as the word being looked up – for example, *independence* and *dependable* as well as *depend*?
- Does it give examples of idioms based on the word being looked up?
- Does it explain any special cultural or sociolinguistic features of the word being looked up? Some words, for example, might only be used in very informal situations.

The precise information that you need to find will vary depending on your target language. Knowing about prepositions after certain verbs, for example, won't be an issue for all languages, whereas information about which gender a noun is (masculine, feminine or neuter) is key for some languages. It is, however, very important that a dictionary gives information that will enable you to use as well as to understand any word you look up.

Over to you

Compare two dictionaries you use or are considering using when studying your target language. You might like to compare a print dictionary and an online one or, if you prefer, you could compare two online or two print ones. Ask yourself the questions above about each of them and note down your answers.

....

....

....

....

If, for both dictionaries, you answered *No* to any of the questions, investigate whether there are any alternative dictionaries or other vocabulary resources available for your target language that could provide you with further information on any words you want to learn more about.

....

34 Language corpora

Many modern dictionaries are based on language corpora. A language corpus is a huge collection of language texts (usually both written and spoken language) brought together digitally. You can search a corpus to find a list of examples of how the word is used. The information is presented along the lines of the example search below for the word *language*, taken from https://www.english-corpora.org/iweb/

2 # 7 # No Second Language **Acquisition** # Second	Language	**Acquisition** is a compulsory module on the M
that they would rather constructors were inherited , making the	language	act as if all derived classes had constructors wi
# How does the provision of a public **service** in another	language	affect a child 's development ? Can differences
means he knows what it 's like to **learn** a new	language	and can deal with many of the practical challer
Language and Culture # Combined **study** of Intermediate	language	and culture . Study of primary sources in print
, with impairments to memory , **visual-spatial** skills ,	language	and decision-making . # Compared to Alzheim
is enough time to train administrators and teachers **on** the new	language	and disciplinary actions outlined in the code ,
to track down a 64DD . He likes **to** study foreign	languages	and enjoys hunting for rare Nintendo collectib
is written in Python , it works well **with** arbitrary programming	languages	and environments , due to the fact that we are
When you do nt feel confident , pay **attention** to body	language	and force yourself to adopt new behaviors . St
will be well placed to pursue the study **of** Old English	language	and literature to a more advanced level . You v

A search like this allows you to see examples of the word in use – the example above is just a small sample of those found under *language*.

A corpus can then be analysed using software such as Sketch Engine (https://www.sketchengine.eu/) to see how language is actually used in practice. It is particularly useful for identifying words that typically appear together in what is sometimes referred to as a cluster.

CLUSTERS (more)	
language •	language in • language arts • language skills • language for • language learning • language learners • language to • language used
• language	english language • foreign language • body language • programming language • second language • other languages • sign language • different langu
language • •	language and culture • language is not • language other than • languages such as • language and literature • languages other than • language used i language and literacy
• • language	in the language • speech and language • in a language • to the language • american sign language • speak the language • in other languages • with th language
language • • •	language other than english • language is not english • languages other than english • language as well as • language in the world • language of the language is not english • languages in the world
• • • language	as a second language • in the english language • as a foreign language • in a foreign language • learning a new language • speakers of other languag a new language • in their own language

Using Sketch Engine and a corpus isn't as complicated as it may perhaps sound. While it may not be worth investigating if you're only learning your target language for holiday travel, it's a useful and fascinating tool for anyone who wants to take their language learning a bit further. It can set you off on a fascinating voyage of discovery.

Over to you

Do a web search for '[target language] language corpus' to find the right corpus for you. Make a note of the name and web address of any corpora you find and what sort of language they contain, e.g. 20 million words, written language only, mainly from newspapers and fiction.

....

....

....

....

....

....

Explore the information on the Sketch Engine website and decide whether you think it's a tool you will use. Experiment with using it by looking up another English word of your choice and noting down what you discover. You can do this by using free access, but you may need to subscribe to use a corpus for your target language.

....

....

....

....

....

....

35 Recording vocabulary

Where to record words

It's important to keep a record of the new words and expressions that you want to learn. The mere act of writing them down will play a part in fixing them in your memory.

Where you store your words will be a matter of personal preference. In Section C, we talked about making a collection of personally useful phrases. You may well want to record useful vocabulary in a similar way. Here are some ideas you might find useful.

- Some people like to have a notebook that they keep in a pocket or handbag for easy access at all times.
- You may prefer a traditional student's file so you can slot in extra pages and move them around according to your current needs.
- Some people choose to write each new word or expression on a separate little card.
- Recording new words in an electronic document has many advantages as it makes it so easy to sort words in different ways and to add new information and examples as time goes by.
- Some people also use a dictionary app which allows them to make a list of words that they have looked up.
- Combining two or more methods can work well too, e.g. a pocket notebook with a computer record.

Revision

However you choose to record vocabulary, the lists you create are vital when it comes to regular revision – we can't overemphasise the importance of regular revision. Revision is for language learning what practising scales is for the piano: an essential part of making progress.

Here are some ideas for revising vocabulary:

- Get into the routine of checking your vocabulary records every week – perhaps on a journey that you make regularly.
- Work with a partner and prepare little tests for each other.
- Add a new example of the word in use each time you revise it.
- Find a way of connecting a set of words you're finding particularly hard to memorise – combining them all in a little story, perhaps.

- Draw a mind map to connect the words you're trying to learn. For example, look at the example below from a learner of English trying to memorise a set of words relating to education.

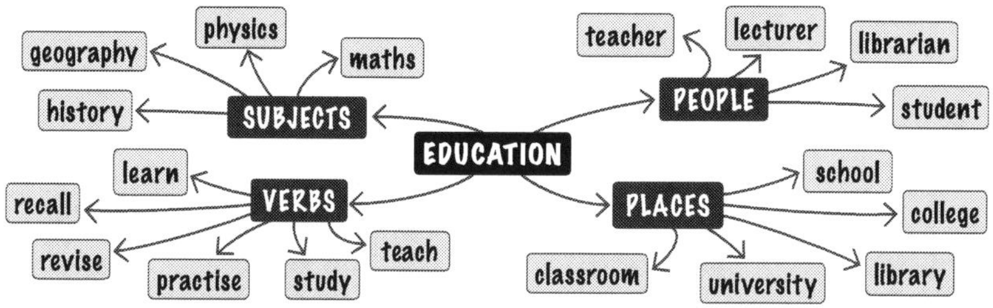

Over to you

How do you record vocabulary now?

....

Is this the most effective way possible?

....

Write down some new words you have learnt recently in the way you think will be most helpful for you.

....

....

....

How do you currently use your vocabulary records when revising?

....

....

....

How could you make more use of your vocabulary records for revision purposes in future?

....

....

....

36 Which vocabulary to record

When deciding which vocabulary items it's worth recording, it may be interesting to consider how frequently a word is used. You can find links to word frequency lists for many languages at this website:
https://en.m.wiktionary.org/wiki/Wiktionary:Frequency_lists

Certainly, it can be useful to know the most high-frequency words for your target language. However, you should be aware that many of the words that top the lists are there because they are grammar words (like *I*, *the* or *it*, for example) and so are probably not needed in your vocabulary lists. Other words are frequent because they are used in so many different ways; the word *way* itself is one of the most frequently used words in English. This is because of the variety of phrases and expressions it can be used in – *by the way, lose your way, get your own way, the best way to make paella, there's no way I'd do that, can you tell me the way to the city centre?* and so on. Clearly, there would be little point in the English learner writing down the word *way* on its own. It's the relevance of the individual expressions that is important rather than the word *way* on its own. It's certainly the case that the same point could also be made about the word frequency list of your target language.

Frequency lists are, of course, not enough on their own. The days of the week, for example, tend not to appear until a long way down such a list. Yet they are certainly words that you will want to learn even at the very beginning of your studies of the language.

Most of the words that you record will come from your textbook or other learning materials you're using or they will be things that you've noticed when reading, watching or listening to something in the target language. You may also find that someone you're speaking to uses a word that you haven't come across before. But you shouldn't write down every new word or expression that you come across when reading, listening or interacting. Focus on those words that you feel it's important for you to know. For example, if you're learning your target language mainly for business purposes then your needs will be rather different from those of someone who primarily wants to use it as a tourist.

See also Tip 57 *How many words do you need?* for information on word frequency lists and reading. See also Tips 34 and 48.

Over to you

What do you expect to be your main needs when selecting which words to write down? Tick the kinds of vocabulary from the list below that you think you will need most:

- vocabulary for tourism
- vocabulary for contact with relatives
- vocabulary used in academic contexts
- vocabulary for business contexts
- vocabulary for other professional purposes
- vocabulary for following the news
- vocabulary for reading fiction
- vocabulary for your hobbies or other leisure purposes

37 It all depends on the context

Noticing words in context

We all know from our own experience, or from observing young children acquire language, that a great deal of vocabulary is picked up from reading or listening to stories or from generally noticing how other people use language. It's the same when learning a foreign language. We can often get a pretty good sense of the meaning of an unfamiliar word from the context in which we come across it.

There are all sorts of clues you can use to help yourself understand an unfamiliar word. You will find the answers to the questions here on page 109.

Surrounding text: Understanding the text that comes before and after the unfamiliar word may give you a fair idea of what the word may mean. For example, what word has *dingle* replaced in this fact?

> For every person in the world there are around 1.6 million ants. The overall weight of all these ants is roughly *dingle* to the combined weight of the world's human population.

https://brightside.me/article/21-crazy-facts-which-you-will-barely-believe-are-true-21755/

Grammar: The sentence where the word is found will probably help you understand whether the word is a verb, a noun, an adjective or an adverb.

> Everyone's fingerprints are unique and so are the prints that would be made by a person's *sompa.*

Is *sompa* a noun, a verb, an adjective or an adverb?

World knowledge: You may have some knowledge of the world that you bring to the context which suggests what the word is likely to mean.

> Tolstoy, famous *lisank* of the novel, *War and Peace*, died of pneumonia while running away from his wife at the age of 82.

Does *lisank* mean reader, author or critic?

In the word: There may be something in the word that reminds you of another word (either from the target language or from another language you know).

> The *likelihood* that the glass of water you're drinking contains a molecule of water that once passed through a dinosaur is about 100%.

If you didn't know the word *likelihood*, what other, more common, English word might help you to understand its meaning?

Get into the habit of using clues like these to work out the meaning of a word before you check it in a dictionary. This will help raise your general awareness of the language you're studying; focusing on the word in this way will also help to fix it in your memory in its context.

Writing down words in context

It's not only important to notice words in their context, it's also important to write them down in their typical contexts. This will make it more likely that you'll be able to start using the words in natural and appropriate ways. Imagine, for example, that you're learning English and have come across this sentence: *The number of people working from home is on the increase as employers are becoming aware of its benefits.* You have decided the noun *increase* would be a useful word to know. Don't note the word *increase* on its own; write down the whole phrase *on the increase.* Then look it up in a good dictionary to find some other examples of the word in use. So you could also usefully note down *an increase in unemployment, a tax increase, a slight increase, an increase of 10%.*

Over to you

Find a short text in your target language, one where you know most but not all of the words. Underline the words you don't know. Use the clues outlined here to work out what the words mean. If all else fails, have a guess.

Check the meanings in a dictionary. How accurate were your predictions?

Write down the words you underlined. Write them in typical phrases as suggested.

....

....

....

....

38 Start with what you know

Learning a language can seem a very daunting task. After all, we continue learning new words in our own language all through our lives. It can, therefore, be encouraging at the start to realise what a lot you probably already know when it comes to vocabulary. Of course, this is particularly obvious if your first language – or another language you've studied – is a Romance language (French, Spanish, Italian or Portuguese, for instance) and you're learning another one in the same group. If you're Swedish you will probably find that you know or can guess many words in another Germanic language such as German, Dutch or Norwegian. If you know English and are planning to learn either a Romance or a Germanic language you will also probably find a lot of familiar words as English has many words in common with both of these language families. However, whatever your first and your target languages, you will find a range of words that are relatively easy to learn because they are already familiar either from your own language or from another language that you know.

Target language words used in your language

Many languages – and English is certainly one of them – are very happy to take in words from other languages to express new concepts. Food and drink words are a typical example. For instance, if you're learning Japanese you probably already know *sushi*, *tempura*, *wasabi*, *bento* and *sake*, while if you're learning Spanish you probably already know *paella*, *tapas*, *tortilla*, *gazpacho*, *chorizo* and *cava*. There is almost certain to be a variety of other words from your target language that you know from your mother tongue. If you're learning Russian, for example, you will easily recognise *cosmonavt*, *sputnik*, *balalaika*, *samovar*, *intelligentsiya* and *vodka*.

Words derived from your language

The language borrowing process works in the other direction too, especially perhaps when your first language is English. Russian, for example, has borrowed such words as *football*, *businessman*, *marketing*, *champion*, *training*, *weekend*, *scanner* and *website*, while German has welcomed in *baby*, *internet* and *software* among others.

It's worth noting that the words you recognise will almost certainly be modified to fit their new environment and so may diverge somewhat in form and/or meaning and/or pronunciation from their English original. Russians, for instance, use the word *boots* for a football boot and add a Russian plural ending when they want to talk about more than one of them (*bootsy*). French uses *le brushing* and *le parking* to mean *blow-dry* and *car park*. It's obviously relatively easy to learn these words despite any slight shifts from their English origins.

International words

There are also bound to be a lot of words that are relatively easy to learn because they are similar in most languages. Words like *bus, taxi, coffee, sandwich, chocolate* and *salad* have recognisable equivalents in most languages, including one as different from English as Cantonese. Words for countries, nationalities and languages are another example. Italy may become *Italija* in Lithuanian, *Italien* in Swedish or even *Taliansko* in Slovak but it still feels familiar. Similarly, Japan is *Japonia* in Polish, *Japonya* in Turkish and *Jepang* in Indonesian. Collecting sets of familiar words like this can be a motivating way to start learning a new language, particularly one that is in other ways very different from your mother tongue.

Beware of false friends

Finally, a word of warning. When you're learning a new language you will probably come across words that look familiar but actually have a very different meaning from what you might have expected. These are known as false friends. There are plenty of examples of US–British English false friends – *I need to change my pants, I like your red suspenders* and *Can you lend me a rubber?* mean quite different things to an American and a Brit. *Pants* and *suspenders* are underwear to a British English speaker, who would use the words *trousers* and *braces* in this context. To an American, a *rubber* is a *condom* whereas to a Brit it's an *eraser*. Examples of false friends for English speakers learning French include *le magasin*, which means *shop* rather than *magazine, la librairie*, which means *bookshop* rather than *library* and *la journée*, which means *day* rather than *journey*. As using false friends inappropriately can cause amusement or even embarrassment, it's worth making a note of these as you discover them.

Over to you

Start collecting lists of each of the following:

- Words from your target language used in your mother tongue

....

....

....

....

....

....

....

- Words from your mother tongue used in your target language

....

....

....

....

....

....

- Words that are very similar in your target and first languages

....

....

....

....

....

....

- False friends

....

....

....

....

....

....

A web search may be able to help you add to these lists. Also, you may have friends who know both languages well and can help you add to the lists.

Keep adding to these lists as you extend your knowledge of your target language.

39 Connecting words with concepts

Learning a new language is all about making new connections in the brain. Your aim should be to start associating the new words you learn with the concept they represent rather than their translation in your first language. So when you see the Portuguese word *beringela* you immediately picture an aubergine in your mind rather than taking the slower route via the English translation of *beringela*.

Picture prompts

You can help yourself to make direct connections between concepts and words by using pictures to help yourself acquire new vocabulary. This method parallels the way that picture books are used to help young children learn their mother tongue. You may be able to find a picture dictionary for your target language which will illustrate words in sets relating to topics such as *clothing, transport* or *in the kitchen*. You may find a useful book of this type that has actually been produced for native speaker children who are learning to read. If you can't find a suitable picture dictionary, why not create your own? Find a large illustration of, say, a bedroom and label all the items in it.

Similarly, make as much use as you can of visuals when you're recording new words in whatever kind of vocabulary notebook you have decided to use. If you're learning the words for *square, circle* and *triangle*, draw the shapes rather than writing the translations. If you're learning *straight hair* and *curly hair*, draw representations to help you learn these words. You don't need to be a great artist; no matter how imperfect you feel your drawings are, they will – psychologists say – help you remember *straight* and *curly* more efficiently than any translation or explanation of those words. Don't limit yourself to nouns and adjectives. You could draw faces to help yourself learn verbs like *smile* or *wink* and stick figures to represent *run, dive* or *kneel*.

Sticky notes

Another popular way to use visual aids for learning is to exploit the genius of the sticky note. Write words for items in your home or workplace and stick them in relevant places. You could label, for example, such things as a wardrobe, a bookshelf, a washing machine, a wall, a printer or a keyboard. Similarly, you could label the outsides of drawers with their contents – socks, scarves, knives, forks and spoons, for instance. It's a good idea to change the sticky notes regularly so you don't stop noticing them. Have a set for, say, 20 different items that you put up for a week or two, then replace them with a set for 20 different items for another couple of weeks before returning to revise your original set.

Other visual aids

Of course, not all vocabulary items lend themselves to visual representation. But some people find they are particularly strong visual learners. If you're one of those, you may find it useful to record vocabulary not just in lists but in more visual ways. You could, for instance, use word forks to illustrate common word combinations (collocations). Here are a couple of examples from English but they work equally well in other languages.

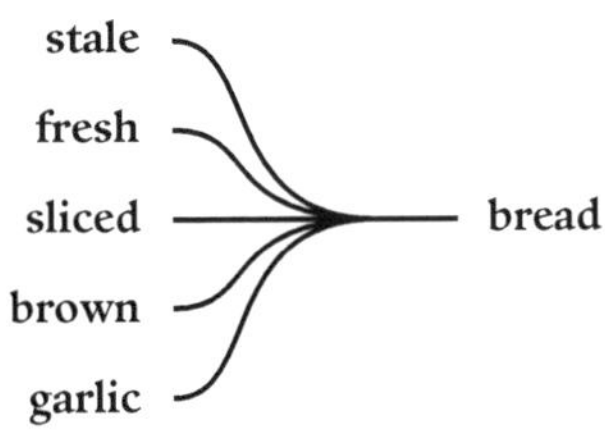

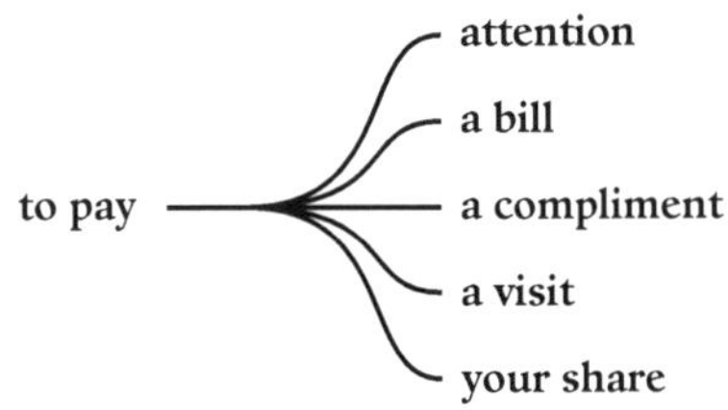

Another way of representing vocabulary in a more visual way is to draw a mind map around a theme, and creating one can be a very good way of revising a set of words related to a topic. You might write a general word – *transport*, for example – in the centre of a page and then draw ovals around that word containing words that relate to that theme. So an oval in the top right corner could contain types of transport, for example, an oval in the bottom left could have parts of a car and other ovals could consist of verbs associated with transport or words related to travelling by train.

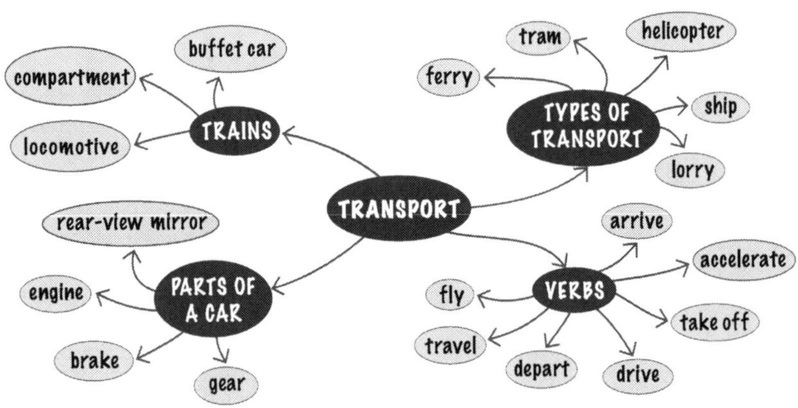

Over to you

Write sticky notes with the target language words for as many things as you can in your home and put them in the relevant places. In this way, you can remind yourself every day of the words for such things as mirror, fridge and keyboard. Don't forget the gender if that's important in your target language.

Draw an example of a word fork for your target language. A dictionary will be helpful when you do this. If you have a friend who knows the language well, they will be able to help you add suitable word combinations.

Draw a mind map of vocabulary in your target language relating to TRANSPORT (or another theme if you prefer).

40 Making connections between words

Research into how language learners remember words suggests that learning sets of words in groups is one of the most powerful ways to help yourself to remember them. There are lots of different ways in which you can group words to this end.

Topic connections

Grouping words by topic is perhaps the most obvious and the most traditional way of organising vocabulary learning and it's one which most people find useful. This can tend to lead to a heavy focus on nouns, so try to remember to include verbs and adjectives as well. If you're gathering words related to food, for example, don't just include types of food, also include some verbs for preparing food (*cook, slice, fry*, etc.) and some adjectives for describing food (*sweet, delicious, fresh*, etc.).

Grammar connections

It can also be useful to group and learn together words that have something grammatical in common. Depending on the particular characteristics of your target language, you might collect groups of:

- nouns that form their plural in an unusual way
- nouns that are different in gender from what you might expect (from either their form or their meaning)
- verbs which share an unusual way of forming their past tense
- verbs which are followed by particular structures.

Word families

By word families we mean words from the same root. In English, examples could be *head, behead, overhead, heading, light-headed, big-headed, headteacher, headland, head first*, etc. Another set of examples in English includes *porter, transport, import, exporter, deport*, etc., all based on the Latin root *port* meaning carry. Thinking about how the current meaning of the word relates to the original meaning of its root will help you to remember the word even if the relationship between the meaning of the word and its root is not immediately obvious.

You could also group sets of words in families that share the same affix. A learner of English, for example, could learn together adjectives that end in *-ful*, or verbs beginning with *mis-* (*misspell, mistranslate, misunderstand*, etc.).

Over to you

Tick the possible topic areas from the list below that you think might be useful for you when learning your target language:

Animals	Food	Politics
Art	Furniture	School
Cars	Geography	Sports
Clothes	Jobs	Weather

Note other topic areas which you would like to build up a collection of vocabulary for.

. . . .

. . . .

. . . .

. . . .

Which of the grammar groupings listed in this tip could be useful when learning your target language? What other grammatical groupings can you think of that would be useful for the language?

. . . .

. . . .

. . . .

. . . .

Would it be appropriate to group words in families in your target language in the way described here? If so, which families will you start by focusing on?

. . . .

. . . .

. . . .

. . . .

41 Personalising words

Research into second language acquisition shows that words that have a personal association for the learner are the most easily recalled. It's a useful tip, therefore, to try to fix words in your own memory by personalising them in some way.

Here is a set of different ideas to help you do this and you will doubtless be able to think of your own variants too.

- If your vocabulary work has had a topic focus, then it's usually straightforward to personalise it. If you've been studying food vocabulary, you could make your next shopping list in your target language. If you've been studying the words for rooms, draw a plan of your home and write the room names on it using your target language. If you've been studying furniture words too, you could add those to the plan. If you've been studying clothing, why not write a list in your target language of the clothes you plan to pack for your next holiday? If you've been learning about places in a town, draw a map of your town and include any relevant words on it.
- When your vocabulary work is based on a reading or listening text, it can be useful to keep a language learning diary. Write a sentence summarising what you have read, listened to or watched in your target language. This will be an initial revision of the language of the text. You can personalise your summary by making a point of adding a note on how you felt about what you read, heard or watched. Another way to personalise your learning diary would be to pick out vocabulary items that you particularly like or that you feel have a relevance for you personally from what you've been studying. In your learning diary you could also note down anything else you wish. You could say how you're feeling about your learning, for example. You could write down any nice bits of language you come across – a proverb or a poem, for example.
- Sometimes vocabulary work focuses on a particular language point. You might want to learn a set of verbs, adjectives or nouns that share one characteristic or another. When that is the case, personalise the language by writing sentences to illustrate those words about yourself or your friends or family. So if you were learning words about sports you might write sentences like *My brother loves skating but I prefer skiing*.
- Imagine you want to learn a set of adjectives for describing people. Don't just write down *thin, tall, friendly* or *lazy*, for example; write also the name of a person you know with that characteristic. When it comes to less complimentary characteristics, it might, of course, be safer to note down

a character from a story or someone in the news rather than a friend or colleague in case your work falls into the wrong hands!

- Sometimes you just have a set of random words and phrases that you want to learn. They could be items that have come from exercises or texts you've been working on recently. Try to incorporate these into a story in some way. It doesn't matter how nonsensical the story is; indeed it's possible that something that is bizarre rather than mundane may be recalled more easily. If your knowledge of your target language is still elementary, you can make up your story in your mother tongue, slotting in the words you want to learn as appropriate. This can be a good activity to do with a fellow learner or two. You could each write a story using the same set of words before comparing to see how differently each of your imaginations has worked. See also Tip 73 *Taking stock and making difficult points stand out* for similar ideas.

Over to you

Which of the personalisation exercises described here do you think you would find most useful? Write down the ones that you plan to try.

....

....

....

....

What vocabulary topic areas have you worked on recently? How could you personalise your learning of the vocabulary for that topic? Try out some of the techniques here for some of these vocabulary topic areas.

....

....

....

....

....

....

....

....

42 Fixing words in your memory

It has been estimated that learners need to meet a word on multiple occasions for it to be fixed in their memory. It seems obvious that the number of times varies. We are convinced that all language learners would agree that some words are easily learnt whereas others simply will not stick. As a rule, however, it's clear that learning words does require effort and you will need to use all the methods you can to facilitate the process.

Here is an example from personal experience: as a child having to learn lists of French vocabulary, the promise of some pocket money for a perfectly recalled set of words for animals or parts of the body was enough of an incentive for me to master vocabulary that I remember decades later. Pocket money might not do it for you now but giving yourself incentives to learn can still be very motivating – you might decide to use your favourite biscuit, a walk round the park or a trip to the cinema to encourage yourself to achieve your next vocabulary learning target.

Revision

There is no avoiding the fact that revision is essential for language learning. One plan would be to look through your vocabulary notes at the end of every day, then at the end of every week and then again at the end of every month.

Nowadays there are apps to help you learn vocabulary for a wide range of languages. They often work by presenting you with the same words over and over again, sometimes in a variety of ways, so that those words eventually get fixed in your memory. Such apps are making use of the power of revision.

If you choose to record vocabulary on little cards with the word or phrase on one side of the card and a translation or definition on the other side, you can then keep an envelope of cards in your pocket or bag and use spare moments on public transport or waiting in a queue to test yourself.

If it's possible for you, you may find it useful to work on revising vocabulary with a friend. Testing each other can often make the process more fun.

Mnemonics

What about those words that you have great difficulty remembering? Why not try creating your own mnemonics or simple phrases to help you? Mnemonics often make use of alliteration and rhyme. Alliteration is when the same initial letters are repeated. *Righty tighty, lefty loosey*, for instance, helps people remember which way to turn a screwdriver when they want to either tighten or loosen a screw. An example of a mnemonic to help with the spelling of *rhythm* is *Rhythm helps your two hips move* – the initial letters of the words represent the spelling of this word which many English speakers find difficult to spell. Another popular mnemonic to remind writers that there are two 'r's in *embarrassed* is *two red cheeks*. When you find a word particularly difficult to learn in your target language, you could try asking a teacher or someone who speaks the language well if they know of any mnemonics that might help you; if not, then why not create your own.

A whole method of language learning has been developed that uses a kind of visual mnemonic to help the learner. This involves thinking of a word or phrase in your native language that resembles the sound of the foreign language word you're trying to learn and then imagining an image linking the two. Thus an English speaker trying to learn the Russian word for juice (*sok*) might imagine a child drinking orange juice out of a sock. It's unlikely to be practical to base your whole language learning round this method but it's undoubtedly worth trying it out when you're finding some words difficult to learn.

Another visual mnemonic technique that some people find extremely effective is called the *loci method*. *Loci* means places in Latin and the method is based on remembering a very familiar journey or place (e.g. your trip to work or your kitchen) and associating what you want to learn with points along that journey or in that place. It's particularly useful if you want to learn a set of items in a list.

Using the words

We all know more words than we actually use in our everyday language. Linguists make a distinction between words in our receptive or passive vocabulary (words that we understand but are unlikely to use ourselves) and words in our productive or active vocabulary (words that we use in our own speaking and writing). If you think that a vocabulary item on your list should become part of your active vocabulary, then you need to make an effort to move it there. This means actually starting to use the words you're trying to learn. Make a point of doing this when you have an opportunity to use your target language, whether it's writing a story for your teacher or having an online chat with a tandem partner or friend.

Over to you

Make a plan for how you're going to build vocabulary revision into your study schedule.

....

....

....

Think of some words that you're having difficulty trying to learn. Invent a mnemonic to help you – it could be based on initial letters, alliteration, rhythm or an image. How effective do you think you personally would find this as a method?

What kind of opportunities can you think of for activating your new vocabulary? List as many possibilities as you can and choose one or two to try out.

43 Beware of homophones and polysemy

We end this section with a warning. Words aren't always what they seem. Many languages contain many examples of homophones and polysemy. These may sound complicated terms but they represent simple but useful concepts in vocabulary learning.

Homophones

Homophones are words that sound the same but are actually different. English has myriad examples including *week* and *weak, pale* and *pail, sea* and *see, right* and *write.*

Remember that words that sound like homophones to you may not actually be so to native speakers of your target language. Here is an example from personal experience: a French boy once asked me, *Why does English have so many different meanings for sheep – the animal, a big boat, not expensive and a bit of fried potato?* He hadn't appreciated that they are actually four distinct words with different pronunciations: *sheep, ship, cheap* and *chip*. So check with a native speaker whether the words you think are homophones actually are!

Polysemy

Polysemy refers to the fact that one word can have multiple distinct meanings. Once again, there are many examples in English. The word *mean,* for example, can refer to the meaning of a word, to being unkind, to being miserly and to an average number. A *bar* can be a metal pole, a place where people drink, a measure in music or something that prevents something from happening. If you read or hear one of the words that has multiple meanings – or hear a homophone – and assume it has the meaning you're familiar with, then you can become very confused. Imagine you only know the English word *mouse* with its small rodent meaning; you will then be puzzled if someone says to you, *Can you remind me to put my mouse in my laptop bag?*

One aspect of polysemy is that words develop new meanings to meet changes in society. *Green* was once just a colour, for example. Then it took on a sense of being inexperienced. Now it's also associated with being environmentally friendly.

Sometimes the different meanings that a word has are clearly related to one another. It's easy to understand why *eye* is also used to refer to the *eye of a needle,* having an *eye for beauty* or the *eye of a storm*. This type of polysemy is particularly likely to be found in your target language.

One of the positive aspects of the abundance of homophones and polysemy in English is that these language features provide the basis for many jokes. Things like *I'm on a seafood diet; every time I see food I eat it* and *Time flies like the wind; fruit flies like a banana* are only possible because of homophones (*sea* and *see*) and polysemy (*flies* as a verb and noun and *like* as a preposition and verb). Similarly, the title of a best-selling book on English punctuation – *Eats, Shoots & Leaves** – hinges on two possible meanings of the word *shoots* (as well as the difference a comma can make).

Over to you

If possible, ask someone who knows your target language well whether it contains examples of homophones and polysemy. It almost certainly does. Note down one or two examples of each.

....

....

....

....

Ask the same person if they can tell you a joke in your target language that is based on either a homophone or a word with multiple meanings. If they can and you can understand it, then you can truly feel proud of your level of understanding of the language. You could also try finding examples of jokes by doing a web search, for example, for 'Russian jokes based on word play' or 'French jokes based on word play'. Although many of the sites this technique leads you to will only give translations, you will also find some sites with jokes in the original language.

If you find an example you like of a joke based on this kind of word play in your target language, note it down.

....

....

....

* See Wikipedia for an explanation of the joke on which this title is based.

Answers

31 The vocabulary of vocabulary

Word	Meaning	Examples
noun	word representing the name of a person, place, thing or idea	tooth, pronunciation
verb	word expressing doing or being	spell, translate
adjective	word describing a person, place, thing or idea	happy, easy
adverb	word describing how something is done or happens	quickly, suddenly
preposition	word that goes before a noun to show how it is related to another word	during, on
idiom	expression with a meaning that is not immediately obvious from the meanings of the individual words in it	sell like hot cakes, keep an eye on
root	most basic part of a word to which other parts can be added	press in *oppressive* and *impression*, help in *unhelpful* and *helpless*
afffix	letter or group of letters added to the beginning of a word (prefix) or its ending (suffix) to make a new word	preview, happiness

37 It all depends on the context

Surrounding text – *dingle* is an adjective and replaced *equal.*

Grammar – *sompa* is a noun and replaced *tongue.*

World knowledge – *lisank* replaced *author.*

In the word – knowing the word *likely* (meaning *probable*) would help with understanding *likelihood.*

Key points

In this section, we have considered ways of learning words and how to remember them. Here are some key points to remember:

- When it comes to communication, vocabulary is the most important part of language learning.
- Learning vocabulary requires regular revision.
- It's worth spending time finding the most suitable tools to help with your vocabulary learning.
- It's important to keep a record of the vocabulary you're learning – in a notebook, in a file or electronically.
- Knowing a word involves a lot more than just knowing what a word means.
- It's important to write words down in typical phrases so that you're able to use them as well as understand them.
- There are a number of different ways in which you can help yourself to remember vocabulary – for instance, by learning words in groups, by associating them with images, and by personalising them in some way.

My own take-home notes on Learning words

....

....

....

....

....

....

....

....

....

....

....

....

....

E Getting to grips with grammar

Grammar, after horse-riding and alongside gardening, is one of the most agreeable sports of all.

Alexandre Vialatte (1901–1971)

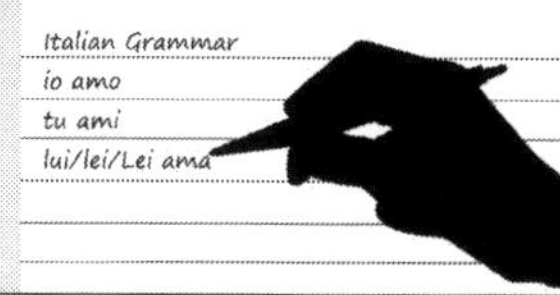

This section helps you focus on the grammar that you need to know when learning a foreign language. The examples we give are mainly based on English but the points we make should apply whatever language you're interested in.

So what is grammar? It's simply the patterns that govern how a language is used. Two such patterns or 'rules' of English grammar are, for example, the fact that most nouns are made plural by adding 's' (*boy/boys, road/roads*) and that most verbs make their past forms by adding 'd' or 'ed' (*imagine/imagined, work/worked*).

Many people don't know very much about the grammar rules that apply in their own language, so is it helpful to think about grammar when you're learning another language? Our answer is 'Yes, but …'. We'll consider why grammar can be useful as well as helping you to avoid some pitfalls. We'll also provide some tips and tricks to help you get to grips with the important bits of grammar in your target language.

Aims of this section

The tips in this section consider:

- whether it's useful to get an overview of the language before you start
- why it's worth considering how much you enjoy learning about grammar.

We also show you:

- how languages used to be taught
- how knowing some grammar will speed up your learning
- some of the terms we use to talk about grammar
- how to find the target language grammar words that are used most frequently
- ways of noticing how grammar is used and how to record it
- how to spot grammatical structures that regularly appear as chunks
- different ways of practising grammar and various resources to help you
- ways of realising how much progress you're making
- how to make your grammar learning personal.

44 Attitudes to grammar

Language teaching in the past

For a long period, the focus of language teaching was on the grammar of the target language. Students were presented with a series of grammar rules. They spent a lot of time in class reciting verb conjugations (*I am, you are, he is, we are, you are, they are*) or doing exercises like making sentences negative. When they weren't doing that, they were usually translating from one language to the other. If they went on to study at a higher level, the focus tended to be above all on the literary classics of the target language. Learning in this way provided students with a good knowledge about the language but relatively little ability to use it in a spontaneous natural way.

In the middle of the 20th century there was a bit of a reaction against this approach. There was a feeling that foreign languages might be better learnt in a way that was closer to the way in which we acquire our own first language. After all, we're fluent in that language long before we consciously learn anything about its grammar. Some teachers even stopped dealing with grammar altogether. The change in attitude can be explained in part by changing social conditions. People were beginning to travel both for holidays and for work and study purposes. They needed to be able to order food in a restaurant or discuss a business deal more than they needed to read literature. In other words, being able to use the language to communicate had become more important than had previously been the case for most people.

Grammar – what is right?

There has also been something of a shift in attitudes towards grammar, particularly among Western linguists. In the past, grammar rules were seen as describing what is right. In English, for example, *between you and I* or *less cars* are often said by native speakers despite the fact that *between you and me* and *fewer cars* are considered more correct. Similarly, dialect varieties of a language often include forms that the standard version of the language would hold to be wrong, and schools tend to correct children who use those forms.

Linguists, however, are more likely now to contend that grammar should be descriptive rather than prescriptive. In other words, grammar should focus on what people actually say rather than on what some expert thinks they should say. After all, it's argued, language changes. In English, the distinction between *less* and *fewer* may well be on its way out, so is there any point in insisting on one form over another? This may make it difficult for a language learner: what kind of grammar should you focus on – should you copy what you hear when it disagrees with what you've been taught? In general, language teaching materials present standard forms of the language and these are usually the safest ones to stick to. We discuss this more in Tip 45.

Over to you

How important has grammar been in your previous language learning? Think about both your first language and any other languages that you've studied.

....

....

....

....

....

....

Can you think of other examples – from any language you know – where people say things that grammar books say are incorrect?

....

....

....

....

....

....

45 A balanced approach

Different personalities and grammar

Some people enjoy studying grammar. They appreciate the attempt to systematise the way language is used. The analytical approach appeals to them. Other people are less enthusiastic, preferring to focus more on other aspects of language learning. Whatever your preferred learning style, we would argue that grammar has an important role in language learning.

Achieving a balance

We believe that your approach to your target language should be balanced. You shouldn't give grammar the excessive importance that it had in the past. Knowing grammar rules alone won't be enough to enable you to communicate. Knowing a lot of vocabulary, on the other hand, may make communication possible. However, if you also have some understanding of grammar rules you will then be able to communicate in a more accurate and appropriate way.

Being accurate

Although the importance of correct grammar may have been overemphasised in the past, being accurate and appropriate in your use of language will help you convey the meaning that you want to convey. A learner of English, for example, will confuse their listener if they say *I'm in London for a week and going home tomorrow*. They would have caused no confusion had they said *I've been in London for a week and am going home tomorrow*.

Native speakers sometimes use non-standard forms of the language and you may well encounter these when listening to everyday speech or song lyrics, as in the Rolling Stones' 1965 hit *I Can't Get No Satisfaction*. However, when you're learning a new language it's safer to stick to what is generally considered standard and correct. You're likely to create a better impression of yourself and of your language ability that way. Therefore, we recommend that you are guided by a good grammar book for learners of your target language. Try to understand and follow the rules that you read there – though also be aware that you're likely to hear native speakers breaking those rules from time to time.

However, while accuracy is undoubtedly a desirable aim, don't let a fear of making mistakes stop you from trying to use your target language. It's only by using the language that you will make real progress with it, so being held back by a reluctance to say something wrong will have a negative impact on how quickly your language improves. Bear in mind that the main thing, after all, is to make yourself understood and in most situations you will be totally clear even if your grammar isn't perfect.

Grammar as a short cut

Learning grammar rules can act as a kind of short cut to acquiring the language. If you know how different tenses are usually formed, then you will be able to use most new verbs that you learn in a whole variety of contexts. If you learn the meaning of, for example, *translate*, you also then immediately have the option to say *I translated, I've translated* and *I'm going to translate.*

It's undoubtedly true that if you spend long enough in an environment where the target language is used, you will probably acquire a feel for its grammar without having to study it formally. However, learning that way is likely to take you much longer than studying a bit of grammar and you may also end up consistently making the same errors without realising it.

Over to you

Answer these questions on a scale from 1 to 5, where 1 means not at all and 5 very much. Note down the reasons why you feel this.

Do you enjoy studying grammar?

....

....

....

Do you feel anxious about speaking a foreign language because you don't want to make mistakes?

....

....

....

If your answer to the second question was 3, 4 or 5, what could you do to stop yourself being held back by such feelings?

....

....

....

46 The vocabulary of grammar

In Section D Tip 31, we looked at some useful terms related to vocabulary. In the box below there are some words that you will come across when you're studying grammar. Other grammar terminology may be needed for specific languages. If, for example, you're learning a language where the noun ending changes depending on its role in the sentence, then you'll need words like *case* and *declension* too. Some languages assign a *gender* (masculine, feminine or neuter) to every noun. If you're learning Chinese or Russian you will need to understand the concept of *aspect* when using verbs (*aspect* means verbs may change their form depending on whether the action is completed or ongoing).

clause	conjunction	future	object
past	phrase	plural	present
sentence	singular	subject	tense

The paragraphs below explain what the words mean. Complete the paragraphs with the words from the box.

One important category in language learning is that of number, which means whether something is [1] .... (i.e. it refers to just one thing) or [2] .... (it refers to more than one). Another basic category is that of time as this affects the [3] .... of a verb, which will be [4] .... if you're talking about now, [5] .... if you're talking about something that is over and [6] .... if you're talking about something that is yet to happen.

In many languages it's easy to recognise a [7] .... in writing because it begins with a capital letter and ends with a full stop. It usually has a main verb, e.g. *drank* in *The cat drank some milk*. It also usually has a [8] .... (*The cat* in the example), which is the person or thing that performs the action of that main verb. It may also have an [9] .... (*some milk* in the example), which is what is affected by the action of the verb.

Some sentences, like the one in the example sentence, are simple but others are more complicated with more than one [10] .... , e.g. *The cat drank the bowl of milk which I put out for her*. (The main one is *The cat drank the bowl of milk* and *which I put out for her* is called subordinate.) A clause always has a main verb in it, e.g. *drank* and *put*. A [11] .... is another term for a group of words that is part of a sentence but it does not include a main verb, e.g. *the bowl of milk*.

Two clauses in a sentence are often connected by a [12] ....
such as *because*, *as soon as* and *but* in the following sentences: *The cat drank the milk quickly because she was very hungry*, *The cat drank the milk as soon as she noticed the bowl* and *The cat drank the milk but wouldn't eat the fish*.

You will find the answers on page 137.

Note that it's useful to know some of the jargon that relates to grammar, but unless your aim is to become an academic linguist, there is probably no need to struggle with a lot of terminology. Only learn those words that are likely to be of practical use when learning your target language.

Over to you

Which of the words presented in the grammar words box have a relevance for your target language?

....

....

....

....

Find a short text in your target language and match as many of the grammar words as possible to examples from the text.

....

....

....

....

47 Getting an overview

The traditional way of approaching grammar involves slowly and steadily making progress by taking one small step after another. However, some people prefer to do things differently; they like to start by trying to get an overview of the grammar of the language before getting down to learning about the details.

Here are some examples from personal experience. One learner we know began her study of Italian by making a poster. She wrote down a common verb (*amare* – to love) in all its different forms, so that she had a big overview showing the complete range of tenses with the endings required by each of the pronouns. Some teachers would criticise this approach as not being communicative enough or as attempting to deal with too much for the brain to handle at one go. However, the aim is not to learn all the forms by heart at this stage but simply to get an impression in advance of what there is to learn. With many languages, an activity like this can also serve to highlight certain patterns in the way verbs are formed – the endings typically used when the verb is used with, say, *I* or *we* or *they* show similarities across a range of tenses.

Another learner was planning to learn as much Mandarin as he could prior to an extended visit to China. He found a website which highlighted the characteristics of Mandarin grammar. It gave him some basic rules, including:

- Chinese words don't change – a verb, for example, is the same regardless of whether it's talking about past, present or future.
- Chinese sentences give prominence to the main topic word, e.g. *soup* is the topic word in the sentence *I love this soup* and so it would feature first in the Chinese translation of the sentence.
- Chinese is very logical. The rules on the whole are consistent without the many exceptions to rules that there are in many other languages.

A similar exercise for Hungarian produced the following summary:

> Hungarian, a highly agglutinative language, uses various affixes, mainly suffixes, to change the meaning of words and their grammatical function. These affixes are mostly attached according to vowel harmony. Verbs are conjugated according to definiteness, tense, mood, person and number.

htpps://en.wikipedia.org/wiki/Hungarian_grammar, accessed September 2020

This is a highly technical paragraph which most of us would require time and a dictionary to get to the bottom of. However, the points about affixes and verb conjugations (i.e. changes in verb forms) show that Hungarian is at the other end of the scale from Chinese, where it seems that words don't change. You may find it useful to be aware of where your target language stands on this continuum right from the start. Alternatively, you might prefer to become aware of it gradually through a step-by-step exploration of the language.

Over to you

Does the idea of getting an overview of your target language before you start studying it appeal to you?

....

....

Try doing a web search on the general characteristics of your target language grammar. Note down any useful points you find.

....

....

....

....

....

....

....

....

48 Focus on what is important

When studying grammar – particularly if you're the kind of person who enjoys analysing language – it's easy to fall into the trap of spending a lot of time and effort on points that have relatively little relevance when it comes to using the language. For someone who is learning English, for example, it seems useful to become confident about using *if* and *unless* but not worth devoting a lot of effort to working out how to use *lest* or *notwithstanding*, as the latter two words are rather old-fashioned and very rarely used.

One way of discovering what is important is to consider frequency lists. We also discuss these in relation to vocabulary (see Tip 36 *Which vocabulary to record*). These are lists of words based on computer analyses of many millions of words of a language in order to see which occur most frequently in the language. Almost all of the 50 most frequent words in English are grammar words rather than vocabulary words. This is not surprising, of course, as grammar words will be found in any context whereas vocabulary words are more restricted in their use.

Here are the 50 most frequent words in English according to a major corpus containing over 100 million words of written and spoken English. They are arranged here in alphabetical rather than frequency order.

a	for	of	to
all	from	on	up
an	has	one	was
and	have	or	we
are	he	out	were
as	her	said	what
at	his	she	which
be	I	that	will
been	if	the	with
but	in	their	would
by	is	there	you
can	it	they	
do	not	this	

http://ucrel.lancs.ac.uk/bncfreq/flists.html, accessed 8 September 2020

Of these words, only *said* can be considered as a content or vocabulary word. All the others function as grammar words – articles like *a* and *the*, pronouns like *I*, *he* and *they*, prepositions like *of*, *by* and *up*, and so on.

A list like this shows just how important it would be for a learner of English to know these words. Of course, knowing these words is in many cases not straightforward. *Which* can be used as a question word, e.g. *Which coat is yours?* or to introduce a relative clause, e.g. *the bus which I take to work ...*; *do* is used in its own right, e.g. *What are you doing?* and to help form questions and negatives, e.g. *What time does your flight land?* and *I don't eat red meat*, as well as in a variety of phrases, e.g. *to do the gardening, do your best, do up a house*; prepositions can also be used in very many different ways. However, getting some sense of the core meaning of each of these words would still be of great advantage to the learner. Fortunately, other words have more distinct roles – *or* and *if*, for instance, are likely to mean much the same whatever context they find themselves in.

Over to you

Can you find a word frequency list for your target language online? If so, you might like to copy it onto your computer or bookmark it.

Write down the web address for the frequency list you find as well as the top 20 words on this list. Then make sure you have some idea of how those 20 words are used.

....

....

....

....

....

....

....

....

....

....

....

....

49 Grammar in context

Learning grammar should not just be a matter of studying form. While some people will certainly find it useful to learn something like a list of irregular verbs by heart, it isn't enough to know what the past form of a verb is, you also have to know what it means and how it's actually used.

An effective way to acquire knowledge about usage is by reading and listening to your target language as much as possible. This, of course, will improve your knowledge of vocabulary as well as your feel for grammar. Reading and listening for pleasure will help you to subconsciously take in grammar patterns, just as you did with your first language. However, you can speed up the process by making a conscious effort to notice the grammar that is being used in the story you're reading or the film you're watching. Ask yourself: What grammar points are illustrated here?

To give an example, what might a learner of English notice on reading this anecdote?

> *The last private owner of the largest house in the area was rather eccentric. She was fiercely protective of her privacy and, when a car-load of sightseers spread their picnic in a corner of her enormous estate, she traced their registration number and gained revenge by having her chauffeur drive her to their suburban home, where she enjoyed her own picnic in their tiny front garden.*

You may have selected other points to notice, but one that stands out is in the phrase *by having her chauffeur drive her* – a structure referred to in grammar books as 'causative have'. It emphasises that you don't do something yourself, you get someone to do it for you; compare *cutting your hair* and *having your hair cut*, for example.

It's easier to notice grammar in this way when you're reading rather than listening, as you can spend as much time as you like looking at a piece of writing. However, it's sometimes possible to get written versions of listening texts that can help you analyse the grammar of spoken language. For example, it's often possible to find transcripts of recordings posted on YouTube (though it's probably advisable to check these – or have them checked – for accuracy). You can also find the scripts of many movies online. When watching a TV programme in your target language, you may be able to switch on the subtitles primarily intended for viewers with hearing difficulties. If you're able to do this, then you will almost certainly notice some interesting differences between the grammar used in speaking and that used when writing.

Over to you

Choose a paragraph from a text in your target language.
What points does it illustrate about the grammar of that language?
Is there anything that puzzles you about the grammar in the text?

. . . .

. . . .

. . . .

. . . .

. . . .

. . . .

. . . .

. . . .

If you noted something puzzling above, ask a teacher or other good speaker of the language or check in reference resources to try to discover why it is as it is. You may find it useful to check more than one reference resource, as one resource may explain things particularly clearly while another may provide some especially good examples.

. . . .

. . . .

. . . .

. . . .

. . . .

. . . .

. . . .

. . . .

50 Recording grammar

The importance of grammar in your learning plan depends on several key factors:

- the complexity of the grammar of your chosen language
- your personal learning context
- the extent to which you enjoy learning grammar and find it helps you in the learning process
- the availability of good resources to help you with the study of grammar in your target language.

However, whether studying grammar takes up a lot of your study time or a relatively small part of it, you will almost certainly find it useful to record some information about grammar. It will be useful for your own future reference but, in addition, the act of writing down key information and examples will play its part in fixing those points in your memory.

You may find it helpful to keep all your grammar notes together in one place – one particular notebook or computer file, for example. You could work towards building your own personalised grammar book dealing with the points that you find most relevant for you, with examples that relate to your own life and experiences. On the other hand, you might prefer not to focus on the distinction between vocabulary and grammar, choosing instead to integrate your notes with those you make on vocabulary or other aspects of your language learning process.

The aspects of grammar that you record will vary considerably depending on your target language. However, there are a couple of recommendations that we would make with regard to making grammar notes. Firstly, you may be basing the notes you make on those you find in a coursebook or other published grammar materials. If that is the case, don't simply copy what you find. If you're learning the present tense of French verbs and your coursebook shows you how the verb *aimer* (to love) is conjugated:

j'aime	nous aimons
tu aimes	vous aimez
il/elle aime	ils/elles aiment

then why not illustrate the conjugation with a different word – *penser* (to think), for instance:

je pense	nous pensons
tu penses	vous pensez
il/elle pense	ils/elles pensent

The second key point to make about recording grammar is to ensure you focus on meaning and usage as well as form. Knowing how a verb is conjugated is fine but you also need to be sure how that verb is used. So include some examples of how the word is used:

J'aime les fraises. (I love strawberries.); *Nous aimons ce restaurant.* (We love this restaurant.)

Tu penses qu'il a raison? (Do you think he's right?); *Je pense que oui.* (I think so.)

Over to you

From what you have already learnt of the grammar of your target language, how complex does it seem to be?

....

....

How might your own personal learning context affect your approach to grammar? For example, if you're going to be studying in a class, it may be more central than if you're mainly acquiring the language through living in a place where it's spoken.

....

....

To what extent do you enjoy learning grammar and feel that it helps you?

....

....

What resources have you got access to that will help you with grammar?

....

....

Where do you plan to record your grammar notes?

....

....

51 Becoming aware of chunks

Computer technology has had a major impact on language learning. It has provided us with easy access to all sorts of texts in whatever language we wish to learn. It allows us to listen to the radio or read newspapers from all over the world. It's given us instant access to dictionaries and other reference resources. It's enabled the creation of a wide variety of apps that can help the language learning process. And it's also offered a wealth of insights into the ways in which languages are actually used.

Computers have facilitated the collection and analysis of language corpora. Language corpora are collections of enormous quantities of text, amounting to many millions of words. As mentioned earlier, in Tip 48 *Focus on what is important*, software is then used to identify patterns of language use. We've already mentioned the word frequency lists which have been produced as a result. The analysis of corpora has also provided us with an awareness of the significance of something often referred to as chunks.

What are chunks?

A chunk is a group of words that very frequently occur together. Chunks often have particular relevance for vocabulary learning. But some chunks have more of a grammar function in that they provide a frame for a sentence.

Examples in English would be:

If I were you, I'd ...
I know what you mean, but ...
I don't know if ...
Having said that, I ...

Such expressions are used in an enormous range of contexts and can continue in countless different ways.

The value of chunks for the language learner is that they provide speakers with a bit of thinking time to work out how best to express the idea that they will go on to convey.

Finding out about chunks

Other languages also make use of chunks and learning them will help you to structure your speech and writing. You will probably be able to use a corpus to get information about your target language as corpora exist for many different languages and are continuing to develop with every year. The TenTen Corpus

Family has collected data for over 35 different languages. The TenTen of its name refers to the fact that the aim is to provide over ten billion words of text per language for analysis. The words in these corpora have mainly been drawn from the internet. Some languages – Russian, Chinese and German, for instance – also offer other corpora which have texts collected from a wider variety of sources. Software such as Sketch Engine will allow you to search your corpus in order to identify groups of, say, four or more words that commonly occur together.

However, it's not necessary to rely only on software. As you read and listen to your target language, you're quite likely to begin to identify chunks yourself. If you do, note them down, as you will be able to make good use of them in your own language production.

Over to you

Find a short text in your target language. Note down any chunks you spot in it. An English learner looking at the two previous paragraphs might note down, for example, *make use of, help you to (do something), get information about, refer to the fact that, allow you to (do something), in order to, rely on, are quite likely to* and *make good use of*. The chunks that you note may well include structures associated with specific verbs and phrases involving specific prepositions.

....

....

....

Search online for a corpus in your target language. What can you discover about how to exploit the corpus? See Tip 34 for more about language corpora.

....

....

If you have already found a corpus, try searching for a chunk of three or four words that you are aware of in your target language. Note down the examples of it in use that the corpus finds for you.

....

....

....

....

52 Getting practice

If you want to be able to apply your knowledge of grammar when interacting with people, it's important to give yourself as much practice as possible. The more you practise your target language, the more you will fix its patterns in your mind. You will, as it were, be creating muscle memory which will gradually make your use of the language automatic.

Here are some things you can do to maximise your opportunities for practice.

Do grammar exercises

You can focus on individual aspects of grammar by doing exercises that deal with points that learners of your target language need to master. You may find these in a book or an app. Try to make sure you work on exercises that are appropriate for your level. Ones that are much too advanced for you are unlikely to be useful. Although a major aim of doing exercises is to make the language they focus on automatic, try not to lose sight of what the language you are manipulating means.

Learn by heart

Learning by heart is more central to education in some cultures than others and has also enjoyed more importance at certain periods of time than others. It's sometimes criticised because you can learn things by rote without having any understanding of what they mean. Despite this, learning by heart does have a place in grammar learning. Depending on your target language, you might want to learn such things as:

- verb conjugations
- lists of irregular verbs
- sets of nouns that share a certain characteristic, e.g. they form their plural in the same irregular way
- sentences that illustrate particular grammar points.

Practise when you write

Make a point of trying to use specific aspects of grammar when you write. For instance, if your teacher asks you to do a piece of writing on a particular topic, then make a conscious effort to use grammar that you've been working on. This will give you useful practice in activating the structure in question. Sometimes you will find that trying to use a specific grammar point makes you realise that you haven't understood it fully, but that is also beneficial in that it encourages you to spend some useful time clarifying the point.

You don't, of course, have to rely on a teacher to provide you with written assignments. You can create your own pieces of writing. You could, for example, write a diary in which you aim to use any new structures you've been studying.

Practise when you speak

Try to stretch yourself grammatically in your target language when you're speaking as well as when you're writing. Once you reach intermediate level (B1 or B2), it's all too easy to remain in your comfort zone. You can get by perfectly well with the structures (and vocabulary too, for that matter) that you've got accustomed to using. So you need to make a conscious effort to activate new language. Although you may feel slightly self-conscious about this at first, you should persevere as you will quickly gain confidence in using this new language too.

Learn from your mistakes

When you practise, you won't get everything right first time but you should try to do what you can to turn your mistakes into a learning experience. Ask your teacher or a good speaker of your target language to tell you when you write or say something wrong, especially if it's a mistake that you frequently make. Correct your mistake and then try to use that piece of language correctly in your next practice.

Over to you

Try out each of the suggestions above in relation to one aspect of grammar that you would like to master.

To what extent in the future are you likely to use each of these approaches to practise the grammar of your target language?

. . . .

. . . .

. . . .

. . . .

. . . .

. . . .

. . . .

. . . .

Note down the importance that each might have for you in your own specific context.

. . . .

. . . .

. . . .

. . . .

Note down some grammar mistakes you know you often make in your target language. Make a plan showing what you're going to do so you stop making those mistakes in future. Remember that getting rid of mistakes is something that takes time; it isn't something that is likely to happen instantly.

. . . .

. . . .

. . . .

. . . .

. . . .

53 Getting help

It's a good idea to use all the help you can get to support your grammar learning. We deal with resources in other tips too (Tips 18, 19, 29, 33, 58 and 63, among others) but here are some of the resources you might find particularly useful when focusing on grammar.

Grammar books

These can range from very complex studies written by academic linguists to simpler presentations aimed more at an elementary learner. Some will be written totally in the target language while others may be about the target language but written in your first language or another language you know well. Some will attempt to cover the language in its entirety while others may focus on one small aspect of it – prepositions or verb forms, for example.

Make sure you work with a grammar book that is appropriate for you. Remember that it's unlikely that your needs will be met by a grammar book that is intended for secondary school pupils who are native speakers of your target language. An English native speaker, for example, doesn't learn about the present perfect or the third conditional in their English grammar lessons at school; they are more likely to spend their time analysing different types of sentence and different types of clauses, differentiating between compound and complex sentences or between adverbial clauses of concession and adverbial clauses of purpose. The ability to make such distinctions is of relatively little value for most people learning English as a foreign language.

Go for a grammar book that focuses on the aspects of your target language that are relevant for you. It could well be that the most useful book for you will have been written with speakers of your first language in mind. Such a book will make helpful comparisons between your language and your target language and should provide plenty of practice in grammar points that are problematic for speakers of your language.

Online resources

There is an ever-increasing range of online resources that you can access, whatever language you're studying or planning to study. You may well find that there are some very good free resources online as some generous language teachers develop resources for their own classes that they then make available online. However, not all of the online resources that you come across will necessarily be sound. You certainly shouldn't waste money on online – or other – materials that promise you can learn a language in a few weeks. Of course, you might learn how to book a hotel room and order a meal in a restaurant in a few weeks but there is no way round the fact that learning a language takes a lot of time and effort. If possible, seek advice from teachers and other language learners about any resources, especially those you are considering purchasing.

Learners' forums

A good way to get advice from other learners is through learners' online forums. Try to find a group that fits your needs. If you can't find one, you could consider setting one up. Such a group can not only share information about resources but members can also help to answer each other's questions about the language.

Other people

Other people who can help you include teachers and learners of the target language who are more advanced than you are. Ask them to help you by correcting your use of your target language. Make sure you agree about how much correction is appropriate. If you're at an elementary level, it would probably be demotivating to have all your errors corrected. It's much better for your corrector to focus on the grammar that you should be mastering at this stage in your learning.

Over to you

Which of these do you already have easy access to for your target language?

- grammar books
- online resources
- a learner forum
- a teacher
- other speakers of the language

....

....

Note what you could do to improve your access to any of these, if you think it would be helpful.

....

....

....

....

54 Making progress

When we think about grammar, what does 'making progress' mean? Of course, learners vary in terms of grammatical accuracy in their use of language depending on their level.

Basic or elementary learners tend to be grammatically inaccurate though they will use certain learnt chunks of language correctly. Intermediate learners are beginning to master the grammar of the language though they will still make plenty of mistakes. On the whole, they are able to find ways to communicate what they want to say even if they don't always do this in the most elegant way. Proficient or advanced learners may still make some errors but these should not usually impede communication. These learners also have a range of language forms at their disposal; they are able to make choices about what might be the best way of communicating their ideas.

To give an example from English, a basic learner might say: *I pass my driving test I very happy*; an intermediate learner might say *If I pass my driving test, I'll be very happy*. An advanced learner would understand the difference in nuance between the intermediate student's statement and *If I passed my driving test, I'd be very happy, If I were to pass my driving test, I'd be very happy* and *Were I to pass my driving test, I'd be very happy*.

So how do you make progress from one level to the next when it comes to grammar? At elementary and intermediate levels, it really is a matter of focusing on learning to use different forms of the language in an accurate and appropriate way by using, for example, your coursebook or grammar exercises. At advanced level, the focus tends to move towards a more sophisticated appreciation of the way grammar can be used to convey subtly different impressions.

Progressing from elementary to intermediate level involves doing all the sorts of things we've discussed in this section – doing lots of practice and getting all the help and support you can from a range of resources. Getting beyond an upper-intermediate level is harder. In fact, many language learners don't need or want to get any further. However, if you do want to progress to an advanced level, you will almost certainly have to read quite widely both in the language and about the language. The only alternative would be to spend an extended period of time in an environment where your target language is used and to remain intensely aware of and curious about the ways in which you hear the language around you being used. Moreover, you would need to make sure that you gain experience of language used in a wide variety of situations and by a wide variety of speakers.

Noticing your progress

It can be hard when you're learning a language to be aware of just how much progress you're making. It's easy to feel you've got stuck and aren't much better than you were several months ago. Here are just a few ideas to help you realise just how far you have come:

- Record yourself speaking every couple of months – talk about a similar topic (how you spent your weekend or a story in the news, for example) – then compare your series of recordings in terms of the grammar structures that you used.
- Keep a record of all the grammar exercises and activities you've done and every now and then look back at these to remind yourself of all your hard work.
- Regularly look back at any work a teacher corrected for you several months ago – you will probably feel that you're now much less likely to make the kind of grammatical errors you were making then.
- Note down a list of grammar points that you would like to feel more confident about and make a plan detailing how you're going to master those points. Set a reminder on your phone for, say, three months' time so you can then revisit your list and hopefully now tick most of the things off it.
- Consider taking a grammar test in your target language as an external, objective way of demonstrating progress.

Over to you

What level do you aspire to achieve in your target language – elementary, intermediate or advanced?

....

How do you plan to make yourself aware of the progress you're making in terms of grammar?

....

....

....

....

....

....

55 Making it personal

Personal examples

As we stated in relation to vocabulary, making language relevant to your own personal situation can help to fix it in your memory. You can do this when it comes to learning grammar too. Imagine you've been learning how to talk about the past in your target language. Write examples about what you did last week or on your last holiday to illustrate the structures you've been studying. Or perhaps you've been talking about making plans. So why not write a couple of New Year resolutions in your target language (even if it's not New Year)?

Diaries

You can write personal examples in a more extended way too. Why not get into the habit of keeping a diary in your target language? If you decide to do this, it can feature the grammar you've been studying too. When writing an entry, make a point of including an example based on the grammar you're currently working on. Here is an example from personal experience: a Japanese learner of English had been working on the third conditional (*If* sentences about the past), so in one diary entry she wrote:

Today I went shopping with a friend. She bought a lovely new pair of shoes. If they'd had them in my size, I'd have bought myself a pair too.'

It can become quite fun trying to find ways of using examples of language you want to learn.

Commonplace books

Wikipedia explains what a commonplace book is as follows:

> **Commonplace books** are a way to compile knowledge, usually by writing information into books. They have been kept from antiquity, and were kept particularly during the Renaissance and in the 19th century. Such books are essentially scrapbooks filled with items of every kind: recipes, quotes, letters, poems, tables of weights and measures, proverbs, prayers, legal formulas. Commonplaces are used by readers, writers, students, and scholars as an aid for remembering useful concepts or facts. Each one is unique to its creator's particular interests but they almost always include passages found in other texts, sometimes accompanied by the compiler's responses.

https://en.wikipedia.org/wiki/Commonplace_book, accessed September 2020

Why not keep a commonplace book 'as an aid for remembering useful concepts or facts' in relation to grammar? Here are some ideas for things that you could include in it:

- lists of words that are similar in some way, e.g. they all form their plural in a characteristic way
- diagrams or other drawings that help to clarify the meaning of something grammatical
- substitution tables that demonstrate sentence patterns – an English learner might include, for example:

I		to school	by bike.
You	go	to work	on the bus.
He/She/It	goes	home	by car.
We		to town	on foot.
They		to the shops	by train.

- sentences that illustrate structures in a way that appeals to you
- paragraphs from stories or other texts that exemplify certain grammar points plus your own responses to these paragraphs.

Over to you

Even if your first response was that these ideas are not for you, try at least one of them out for at least a month. If you can integrate it/them into your language learning habits, we are sure you will find it both enjoyable and useful.

Which idea are you going to try out first?

....

....

....

After trying it, note down whether you found it useful and enjoyable.

....

....

....

Answers

46 The vocabulary of grammar

One important category in language learning is that of number, which means whether something is [1] **singular** (i.e. it refers to just one thing) or [2] **plural** (it refers to more than one). Another basic category is that of time as this affects the [3] **tense** of a verb, which will be [4] **present** if you're talking about now, [5] **past** if you're talking about something that is over and [6] **future** if you're talking about something that is yet to happen.

In many languages it's easy to recognise a [7] **sentence** in writing because it begins with a capital letter and ends with a full stop. It usually has a main verb, e.g. *drank* in *The cat drank some milk*. It also usually has a [8] **subject** (*The cat* in the example), which is the person or thing that performs the action of that main verb. It may also have an [9] **object** (*some milk* in the example), which is what is affected by the action of the verb.

Some sentences, like the one in the example sentence, are simple but others are more complicated with more than one [10] **clause**, e.g. *The cat drank the bowl of milk which I put out for her*. (The main one is *The cat drank the bowl of milk* and *which I put out for her* is called subordinate.) A clause always has a main verb in it, e.g. *drank* and *put*. A [11] **phrase** is another term for a group of words that is part of a sentence but it does not include a main verb, e.g. *the bowl of milk*.

Two clauses in a sentence are often connected by a [12] **conjunction** such as *because*, *as soon as* and *but* in the following sentences: *The cat drank the milk quickly because she was very hungry, The cat drank the milk as soon as she noticed the bowl* and *The cat drank the milk but wouldn't eat the fish*.

Key points

In this section, we have considered ways of getting to grips with grammar. Here are some key points to remember:

- Your approach to learning grammar will depend to some extent on your individual circumstances (including your target language, your learning context and your individual preferences).
- You should remember that while some focus on form may well be important, this should always be related to how those forms are actually used in practice.
- To help yourself learn grammar efficiently, you should try to become aware of how it's being used when you're reading or listening to your target language.
- The importance of getting lots of practice, of personalising the language you're studying and of making good use of resources and other forms of support are all as important when it comes to grammar as they are for vocabulary.

My own take-home notes on Getting to grips with grammar

....

....

....

....

....

....

....

....

....

....

....

....

....

F Improving understanding

Man does not live on bread alone, my friend, but only completely by developing his critical skills and understanding.
George Sand (1804–1876)

In this section, we focus on understanding authentic language or language found in real contexts, rather than language that is sometimes simplified or presented in single sentences or very short texts in classroom contexts.

The more you understand, the faster your progress and the greater your confidence in the target language becomes. So improving your understanding of the spoken and written word can be a fast track to overall progress. This doesn't mean you will be able to understand a novel or film when you begin learning a language, but you will be able to read short articles in a newspaper or understand commercials on television surprisingly quickly.

Aims of this section

The tips in this section show you:

- why it's important to read with an aim in mind and be aware of how you're reading
- how to find the most useful vocabulary
- how reading helps vocabulary building
- how different approaches to reading can affect your progress
- why listening is so often difficult and how to improve your listening comprehension
- where to find sources of listening materials and how to use them
- how to use feedback to improve speaking and understanding
- how to make the most of learning with a tandem partner.

56 What makes a good reader in a foreign language?

Even if you're a good reader in your own language and you read a lot, you may find reading in a foreign language challenging, whether you're a beginner or an advanced learner. Research into second language reading shows that when adults find reading difficult in a foreign language, they may slide into poor reading habits. For example, they may get stuck on a difficult word they don't understand and lose sense of the overall meaning of the text.

Here are some of the factors affecting the way we read and skills we can apply in tackling texts.

Adapting the way you read to your reason for reading

There are many different reasons for reading. We read for information when following instructions, such as making a cake or changing a tyre. We read novels, blogs or magazines about our hobbies for entertainment. Reading often takes up a lot of time at work and when studying, and we read emails and other texts in personal interaction as well. When we read newspapers or reviews, we are interested in other people's opinions and, of course, we read and study information before making important purchases.

However, we don't approach different types of reading in the same way. If we're reading a list of ingredients on a food product to ensure it doesn't contain additives, we're reading for specific information and will quickly 'scan' through parts of the text to find this. We won't waste time reading everything on the packet. However, if we're reading an article in a journal such as *The Economist* or *Scientific American*, we may first 'skim' it to get the main ideas, for example by reading the title and subtitle, then the first and last paragraphs and section headings. Then, if we feel it's relevant to our needs and/or interests, we read through the whole article for detailed understanding. These are examples of approaches we adopt without thinking in our own language but may fail to use in a foreign language.

Text types and structure

The overall structure of texts is not always the same in different languages. In English, for example, the main idea in a text such as an essay or critical article is usually presented in the first couple of paragraphs. The idea is then developed over a number of paragraphs and finally often summarised near the end of the text. If you understand the way texts are built in your target language, it makes finding key information and overall understanding easier.

The writer's attitude

You may also want to consider the writer's attitude, for example, at beginner level if reading a travel guide, or at a more advanced level, a journalist's political views. Does the writer have a generally positive or negative view of the topic? Is he or she being serious, humorous or possibly manipulative? To get an idea of the writer's slant, your knowledge of vocabulary will help you at all levels. At a more advanced level, it will also help to stand back and consider the arguments the writer uses to back his or her claims and the way the argument is constructed.

Over to you

Find one or two texts from a text type you usually read or are likely to read. You can use very short texts if you're just beginning the language. It's important to choose texts to read that are not only interesting or meet your individual needs, but that are also relatively easy to read at your current level.

Find another very different text type, e.g. a recipe or other instructions. Consider whether you can read this in the same way as the other text(s) or if you need to adapt your approach.

Does this have an impact on your learning? Make some notes below.

....

....

....

....

....

....

....

....

57 How many words do you need?

Let's take English as an example. Linguists estimate that there are 54,000 word families in English. A word family includes the base word and its derivatives, e.g. *stimulate + stimulated, stimulates, stimulating, stimulation* and *stimulant*. A native speaker who is a university graduate probably knows about 20,000 word families, although there is a lot of variation between individuals. Many adult learners of English as a foreign language have a vocabulary of about 5,000 word families, often after studying English for several years.

But learners of English shouldn't be daunted; with only 2,000 words, you can understand 80% of most articles in a newspaper, and almost 90% of a lot of fiction. These magical 2,000 words were identified back in the 1950s, but the list has remained very relevant as they are everyday words in English. We wouldn't suggest English learners should work through a list; for most learners it would be tedious and ineffective. However, a lot of vocabulary learning books for many foreign languages are based on the most common words in those languages and working through such a vocabulary book can help learners to master those words relatively quickly.

If the English learner's level is advanced, another word list could help them to expand their formal vocabulary and increase their understanding of more complex texts. The Academic Word List (AWL) is based on 570 words that are not in the original list of 2,000 words. The list was developed to help students studying in English whose mother tongue was not English. However, the words in the lists are not specific to particular academic disciplines and tend to occur not only in academic texts but also in quality newspapers and any formal written texts. The big advantage of the Academic Word List is that a lot of exercises are available online to help students learn and practise the words.

You can find links to word frequency for other languages at:
https://en.m.wiktionary.org/wiki/Wiktionary:Frequency_lists

It's important to work on everyday vocabulary first. You can start with as few as two or three words a day. Pick the words you come across when reading or listening that seem most useful to you. If you're out of practice trying to memorise things, this will be very helpful and you'll be surprised to see how quickly you build up to memorising ten or 12 words a day. Of course, you do need to keep going back over the words; try to notice them when you're listening or reading.

See Tip 36 *Which vocabulary to record* for more information about frequency lists.
See also Tips 34 and 48.

Over to you

Beginners and intermediate learners

Do some research to find free online vocabulary learning exercises that are based on everyday themes and have exercises based on texts at your level. You may also find useful apps. Try some of them out. If you prefer working with a book, see what is available for your target language.

Advanced learners

If you're learning English, you may find the AWL interesting. If you're learning another language, look at the Wiktionary link for frequency links and do a web search for 'online exercises in [your target language]'.

Learners at any level

Try to find texts with accompanying exercises that put the words in a meaningful context and allow you to practise the same words in different ways, so that you don't forget them.

58 Links between reading and vocabulary

Some specialists believe you need to build up a good level of vocabulary before you start reading authentic texts, while others feel that reading as much as you can and as soon as you can helps you to increase your vocabulary. There is probably some truth in both of these views.

Both views point to the fact that vocabulary is central to learning and using languages, as outlined in Section D on vocabulary. Clearly, you won't be able to read the newspaper if you only know a few words, but you might be able to read the menu in a restaurant.

Intensive and extensive approaches to reading and vocabulary learning

Intensive work on vocabulary is valuable, particularly in the early stages of language learning, and can also be helpful when seeking to master specific areas of language such as the language of economics or academic language. At an advanced level, when you already have a big vocabulary, spending time actively identifying and learning unknown words instead of just skipping over them is worthwhile.

Traditional vocabulary instruction involves focusing consciously on words, their definitions, word grammar, etc. This helps build depth of meaning and can be achieved by intensively reading and working on vocabulary in short texts, from a paragraph to a page. On the other hand, learning vocabulary through extensive reading of a much longer text is indirect in that the focus is more on the meaning of the whole text rather than on individual words, so that vocabulary is gradually assimilated rather than deliberately studied.

Some studies of native-speaking children learning to read show that while their vocabulary can grow by over 1,000 words a year, only a small proportion of these words will be consciously studied in class. It is through extensive reading, and indeed listening, that the exponential growth occurs. The value of expanding your vocabulary through extensive reading is that you're encountering words in context multiple times, drawing on contextual information in the texts and your knowledge of the world to build up your understanding. All these factors help to fix the new vocabulary in your brain.

Over to you

What do you like reading? For extensive reading, you ideally need a page turner. This might be a thriller, a book on sport or a love story. However, it may have to be an academic article that you need to read.

Start reading extensively. Read for at least 15 minutes to 'get into' the text. If you really don't like the text and you have a choice, look for another text. Don't look up any words in your first session. You'll be surprised how much you understand!

59 Exploiting reading resources

In Section B, we reviewed language learning resources, including for reading. Here, we look at some of the ways you can draw on such resources and take different approaches to improve your understanding.

Extensive reading – reading a lot, focusing on meaning

If you're reading for pleasure in your target language, you can simply read and enjoy! You could:

- seek out the kind of texts you read in your own language, but read them in the target language
- reread a book such as a novel you have already read in your own language
- experiment with a new genre – spy or crime novels, short stories or poetry; ask for guidance in a bookshop or public library or on an online forum
- read bilingual books, where the text appears in the target language on one page and in translation on the opposite page.

If you're reading for business or study, you may not have a choice of texts, although you may be reading a lot. However, unlike reading for pure pleasure you may have to work on the texts in some way; your focus will still be on meaning though rather than the language per se. You could:

- highlight or underline key passages
- write out short summaries of key ideas for revision or presentation to colleagues
- make notes in the margins on the main ideas or even invent potential exam questions.

Either way, don't get stuck on individual words or be tempted to look up every word you don't understand.

One word of warning: unless you're at an advanced level, avoid books written a very long time ago. The language may no longer be like contemporary language and won't help you so much in language learning. The way people speak often changes over time, so it's better to read contemporary texts with language that you can use and that will sound natural.

Intensive reading – short bursts of reading for learning

For intensive reading, you may choose to work on a short section, say a couple of paragraphs from a longer article, a page from a novel, a short newspaper article or a text from a website. Whatever you choose, it should be relevant in terms of:

- **Vocabulary** – focusing on words that are worth learning is important; you may recognise them but be unsure of their meaning or know what they mean, but not yet use them, or they may be completely new to you.
- **Grammar** – highlighting or underlining grammar points that you either don't understand, feel you're beginning to grasp, or need to work on more is worthwhile at any level. Having identified them, you can refer to your grammar book or do online exercises to work on them. You may also feel you need guidance and explanations from your teacher.
- **Text structure** – focusing on structure works with most texts and can be helpful in making complex texts clearer if you're a more advanced learner. There is more information on this in Tip 60 *Intensive reading exercises*.

To summarise, here are some points to bear in mind:

- wherever possible, read what you enjoy and can't wait to continue reading!
- read what you find reasonably easy for your level
- don't expect to understand every word when reading unless you're focusing on a short text for intensive reading
- introduce variety to the types of texts you read and the sources.

Over to you

This is an example of a mind map that identifies some of the main text types one of the authors reads.

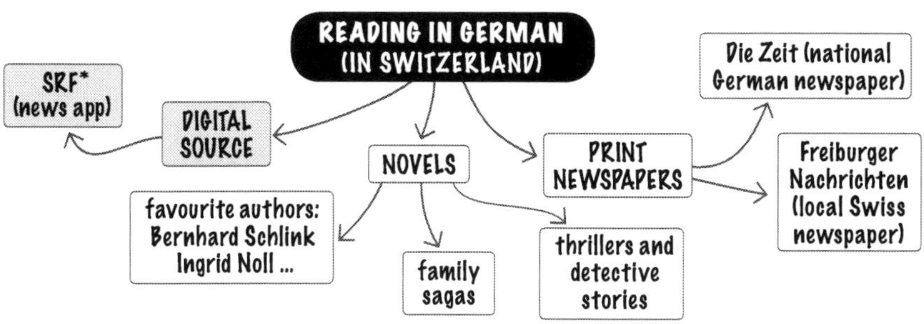

* Schweizer Radio und Fernsehen (SRF): official Swiss German-speaking broadcaster

Draw a mind map showing what kind of texts you currently read. See Tips 35 and 39 for other examples of mind maps.

Your mind map:

Take a coloured pen or highlighter and highlight some of the text types on your mind map that you want to read next in your target language.

Make your choice and start reading! If you find it difficult, don't give up at once. If you don't like the topic, then consider moving on to something more motivating.

60 Intensive reading exercises

As we outlined in Tip 58 *Links between reading and vocabulary*, working intensively on short texts allows you to build depth of knowledge of words, going beyond definitions to study aspects of vocabulary such as word grammar or pronunciation. This is more likely to help you remember new words or begin to use words you recognise but haven't yet used actively. See Tip 32 *What does knowing a word mean?*

We advise learners at different levels to work on different lengths of text: a sentence or short text for beginners, a paragraph for intermediate learners, up to a full page for advanced learners.

In Tip 59 *Exploiting reading resources*, we noted that intensive reading can involve focusing on vocabulary or grammar within a text. Here, we give examples of exercises that can raise your awareness of these aspects of language:

- vocabulary
- grammar
- text structure
- the writer's attitude
- finding out how to 'do' things in a different culture.

Here are some sample exercises.

Intensive work on vocabulary

A sentence to analyse for someone learning English:

> At the end of my first German lesson my mouth ached.

- highlight or underline a useful phrase, e.g. *at the end of*
- look up the phrase in an online dictionary or app and see what phrases with the same or a similar meaning come up
- see how they are used in context
- try to use the phrases when speaking
- identify words you don't understand, e.g. *ache*. Look them up to see what other expressions are used with the word or words (*toothache, headache*). *Ache* is a good example of a word that isn't pronounced the way it's written. Online dictionaries and apps allow you to listen to the pronunciation – take advantage of this! Then make notes to learn the words and expressions.

You can see that with just a sentence you can work intensively on vocabulary, so don't be over-ambitious. Just work on a little at a time.

Intensive work on grammar

Lorsque j'ai commencé à apprendre le français, j'avais huit ans. Au début, nous n'avons appris que du vocabulaire. Lors de la première leçon, nous avons dégusté du saucisson et du pâté. Je n'oublierai jamais cette expérience, c'était très motivant et une bonne idée du professeur.

When I started learning French, I was eight. In the beginning we only learnt vocabulary. In the first lesson, we tasted (French) sausage and pâté. I'll never forget that experience, it was very motivating and a good idea of the teacher's.

There are many ways one could exploit this text, but here, the underlined words indicate the gender of different nouns and also adjectives that change their form if the noun is masculine or feminine. The gender of words has to be learnt with the words and actively highlighting or underlining them when working intensively on a text can help you either confirm that you have learnt the gender of a word correctly or, if the word is new for you, you can make sure you learn it with its correct gender.

This short text could also be used to work on verb tenses, but it would only make sense if you were working on tenses at the time or needed to improve your grammar in that area. It's better to focus on one or two aspects of grammar and keep the exercise short!

Intensive work on text structure

In the following paragraph, the first sentence introduces the subject 'language learning'. The writer then contrasts difficulties adults can have learning a foreign language with children's ease when immersed in the language. The writer thus presents a balanced argument before finally introducing his or her own opinion, i.e. that learning a foreign language is worth the effort.

Identifying the way the writer develops his or her argument can help improve understanding. Shades of meaning can also be identified, reflecting the writer's attitude, when one considers the choice of words: are they positive, negative or neutral?

> Language learning can be challenging, particularly for adults. Some people may not have had the opportunity to learn a language at school and may not know how to approach language learning later in life. Or, they may not have enough time to work regularly on the language. In contrast, children immersed in a foreign language learn very quickly. However, language learning is stimulating at any age and well worth the effort!

Identifying so-called 'signposts' can be helpful in understanding both written and spoken texts. In the short paragraph below, the signpost words are underlined, helping the reader to create a mental map that guides him or her through the text.

> Many children want to have pets and there are a number of reasons to buy or not to buy a child a pet. Firstly, looking after the pet can help the child build a sense of responsibility. Secondly, children and pets often bond, developing a deep relationship, so a dog, for example, can become a welcome playmate. On the other hand, the parents often end up doing the everyday chores relating to pet care. Finally, not all pets may be suitable for small children, notably in terms of safety.

In the text, the author mentions *a number of reasons* so the reader knows that there will be more than one. The advantages are listed with *Firstly* and *Secondly*. *On the other hand,* indicating contrast, then introduces the first reason against buying a pet for a child and *Finally* the second reason, highlighting possible danger with the word *notably*.

Highlighting, or underlining, and analysing signpost words can help you not only to understand a text better, but also to expand your own range of such useful words.

Intensive work on cultural differences

Much everyday written communication has become more informal over time, which makes it easier in some ways in a foreign language.

Here is an example from personal experience of a short note. It was sent as a follow-up to a meeting between one of the authors and an insurance salesman, in which they discussed a contract. The salesman sent the final version of the contract to sign and return. In the French-speaking Swiss context, insurance companies tend to be reasonably formal, but adopt a friendly tone. A more formal tone often would be used in letters.

Madame Pullin,
Suite à notre agréable rencontre, merci de me signer et retourner la proposition avec l'envelope retour.
Je reste à votre disposition en cas de questions.
Meilleures salutations.
ABC Compagnie d'assurances

Dear Ms Pullin,
In follow-up to our pleasant meeting, may I ask you to sign and return the proposal in the enclosed envelope.
Please don't hesitate to contact me if you have any questions.
Kind regards,
ABC Insurance Company

In this example, the relationship is professional, so the writer uses a title and family name. This might, of course, differ considerably from one culture to another or indeed in different corporate cultures, which may be more or less formal. Mentioning an 'agréable rencontre' or 'pleasant meeting', creates a friendly tone, although it could be inappropriate in some contexts! Much of the language here is formulaic and could be noted for later use if you need to write emails, notes or letters for business purposes. The closing phrase 'Meilleures salutations' could be useful in many contexts.

Adopting an appropriate level of formality is important. If you're too formal, you may appear distant or even superior, whereas language that is too informal can give the impression of overfamiliarity or a lack of professionalism in business contexts.

Over to you

Choose a short text or a paragraph from a text, for example from the BBC News website if your target language is English. Note down the title or source of the text.

....

....

What does the text contain that interests you in terms of the following? Write some notes alongside or in the text itself, or here. Base your notes on these categories:

Vocabulary

Grammar

Cultural content

Text structure

The writer's attitude

To improve your awareness of cultural differences in communication, collect written messages you receive. In addition to highlighting or underlining key phrases and possibly copying them into a database for future use, you could also make notes on them concerning:

- the context and subject, either professional or personal
- the sender's relationship to you
- how formal or informal the language is.

61 What makes listening difficult?

When you begin to develop rudiments of a language and can, for example, order a meal in a restaurant or ask for directions in the street, it can be a shock to find that you can't understand anything that is said to you in response! Even at an advanced level, listening can be frustrating as you want to understand everything but often you can't.

The nature of speech

Apart from speed and accents, the nature of speech itself makes understanding challenging in a foreign language. When reading, you can go back and reread something you haven't understood; usually this isn't possible with speech. When people interact with each other naturally, speech can be 'messy'. Speakers interrupt and overlap each other, backtrack, change the subject or digress, and all this is a natural part of conversation. People also have different styles when speaking. Some speak very fast, in which case you might find it difficult to identify individual words. Some people, on the other hand, speak quite slowly, which can be very helpful for language learners.

Here are some of the reasons learners give for finding listening comprehension difficult:

- people seem to speak too fast
- there is too much information to assimilate
- the speaker has an unfamiliar accent
- the speaker refers to unfamiliar people, places or things.

Coping strategies

There are some initial solutions:

- first of all, don't panic or 'switch off'. Memorise some phrases such as *Could you repeat that more slowly, please?* or *Could you say that again with different words, please?*
- focus on getting a general understanding initially
- don't expect to understand every single word. We don't always understand everything in our own language.

As your vocabulary expands and you gain exposure to different accents, you will gradually understand more and more. When you first start learning the language, you may be able to recognise individual words such as *Hello* when speaking. As you progress, you will find that you can pick up phrases such as *How are you?*

As you reach intermediate level, you will be able to understand the main ideas, for example on the news, and begin to understand some detail with further practice and as your vocabulary expands. At an advanced level, you can expect to understand as much detail as many native speakers and also be aware of speakers' attitudes and implicit messages. Of course, your level of understanding will also depend on who is speaking and in what context, as well as your knowledge of the subject. After all, many native speakers wouldn't understand a specialist university lecture, for example, on physics.

But whatever stage you're at, remember that regular listening to your target language, even if it's only five minutes every morning when you get ready in the bathroom, will have a positive impact on your listening comprehension – and your confidence!

Over to you

Find a very short source of listening. For example, for learners of English the BBC Learning English website has listening texts as short as one minute. YouTube has a huge variety and you can select the length of the videos. You might like to make a note of the best sources you find.

....

....

....

....

....

Listen to a short recording from one of your sources and consider the difficulties and coping strategies above in relation to the way you approach listening.

What can you learn from this?

....

....

....

....

....

62 Improving listening comprehension

Here, we look at ways to actively improve your listening comprehension over time.

Plan regular time slots for listening comprehension. These can be as short as five minutes if you listen to a news summary, review the main points in your head and then listen again to try to understand more, or simply move on. Doing this every day or several days a week will definitely help improve your understanding. As you progress, you can also watch films or documentaries, for example.

Determine your reason for listening beforehand. This will also depend on your level. If you're a beginner, you may just want to understand the key points, for example in the weather forecast. If you're more advanced, you may wish to take notes if you're watching an online lecture, or simply sit back and enjoy a film.

Think about and choose what you want to listen to carefully, depending on your level and needs. Work on the topic before you listen. If you're going to watch a lecture, you will probably already have some knowledge of the topic. Reviewing this beforehand and possibly doing some reading around the subject will reinforce your understanding when you listen or watch. At a lower level, study related vocabulary before listening and if you can watch something rather than just listen, seeing the speaker in context can also help.

Do a task while listening. If you're a beginner, this could be simply writing down words you recognise when listening, or if you're advanced, it might be writing down expressions you don't know. Doing a task will help focus your attention and increase understanding. If you're watching a film, you might just want to enjoy it, and then you could go back over the plot in your head afterwards or tell someone about it in the target language.

Listen and read at the same time. You could do this with an audiobook, for example, or you may be able to read the text at the same time as watching a video of, say, a talk or a song, on YouTube. This can be helpful in giving you a feel for the language's natural melody.

Measure your progress

From time to time, it's a good idea to assess how much you have understood after listening. You can do this simply by guesstimating the percentage you understood. Listening to short recordings twice can help you to understand more and thus be motivating. With films or similar longer recordings, you could watch them or listen to them again after a few weeks or months, which can help you to see that you're making progress.

For some languages you can buy books specifically focusing on listening, with a range of activities and comprehension questions. Working through such a book can help you to make systematic, gradual progress and see exactly what and how much you really understand. Similarly, there are such listening materials online.

Over to you

Consider how you can integrate listening into your daily or weekly routine. Could this be in the car or on public transport going to work or while cooking at home?

....

....

....

....

What do you want to listen to?

....

....

....

....

When will you practise listening?

....

....

....

....

What do you need to do before you start and when will you start?

....

....

....

....

63 How to use listening sources

Do you like watching documentaries or listening to podcasts on history or politics? Perhaps you like lighter viewing such as short YouTube videos on football, cookery or pets? Maybe you need to improve your listening skills to study at university abroad? We all have different tastes and needs but most sources of listening can be used to improve comprehension.

It's important to choose sources and subjects that you find really interesting so that you genuinely want to understand the speaker and will want to listen to more.

Short sessions

Listening or viewing material that is short, say between 30 seconds and four minutes, can be suitable for any level. For beginners, it helps to have some visual support to show the context and also subtitles or an audioscript. On the other hand, for advanced learners listening to the radio or podcasts with no visual support can provide a suitable challenge, as can listening to speakers with a range of accents or watching TV dramas where people interact in groups.

Some public broadcasting companies, such as the BBC and Deutsche Welle, have excellent listening lessons based on short audio or video recordings, with comprehension questions, the audioscript and vocabulary work. They are usually designed for specific learner levels.

Here are some ideas for working with the news or short audio or video recordings on a range of topics:

- if you're just beginning, watch very short videos and try to find ones with subtitles whenever possible
- try to find something designed for learners, such as listening tasks for English on the BBC website
- plan regular short listening activities
- if your level is intermediate or higher, find YouTube tutorials and perhaps slow down the speed (see below for how to do this)
- listen to the news or a news summary in your own language and then in your target language
- study the vocabulary relating to a particular topic and then watch a video on that topic
- take notes while listening and then summarise what you learnt to another person

- note down words you don't understand, look them up and begin learning them; this is more helpful at an advanced level, when you may find that there are only a few words you don't understand.

Longer sessions

If you're a beginner, it's best to keep your listening sessions short. At intermediate and more advanced levels, you will be able to listen for longer.

Intermediate – choose something you find interesting. Study related vocabulary first. Practise summarising the key points after listening and listen several times. Documentaries can offer relatively easy longer listening sessions. They can be easier to understand than drama or comedy as the aim is usually to explain something clearly and the film provides the context.

Advanced – challenge yourself! Choose something you would listen to in your own language such as the news or a spy drama. Note down and look up key words you didn't understand. Keep at it!

Much of the time, just listening and focusing on the content will help to improve your understanding.

For longer, more challenging listening, you could listen to a TED Talk (https://www.ted.com/) or a podcast. If you enjoy listening to audiobooks in your own language, try one in your target language.

If you're a cinephile, going to the cinema regularly is a wonderful way of improving listening comprehension. If you can't go to the cinema, you can find many foreign language films online or, if you have the opportunity, subscribe to a streaming service. You can also borrow films from your library. Foreign language films often have subtitles. You can choose to look at these or not.

You could even sign up for a MOOC (Massive Open Online Course), which may involve some listening, although many courses will comprise more reading. You can search for courses in numerous languages (https://www.mooc-list.com/languages). University websites often include a lot of interesting content for listening as well as opportunities to learn online.

If you like visiting museums, many of the world's major museums, such as the Louvre in Paris and the Hermitage in St Petersburg, offer online guided tours of their collections.

YouTube has an infinite number of audio and video recordings for listening practice. It's easy to make listening easier by using the tools they provide: open YouTube on your computer, tablet or phone, search for a subject that interests you and open a video of your choice. You can filter for 'short videos' and ones of any length. If you click on the settings button at the bottom of the screen, this will allow you to have subtitles and also run the video at a slower speed. If you click on the three horizontal dots under the screen to the right of Save, you can access the full transcript.

Over to you

Try out some of the ideas above. Depending on your level, try a short listening session or a longer one. Make some notes on what you found most interesting and helpful.

....

....

....

....

....

Listen to a range of audio sources. For example, watch a film trailer or listen to a podcast relating to your hobby, or choose a YouTube video. Practise watching it with the transcript or subtitles (if available).

....

....

....

....

....

You might like to set up a library of interesting viewing/listening materials on your computer, tablet or phone to watch or listen to again later. If so, note down some preliminary ideas.

....

....

....

....

....

64 Speaking and the importance of feedback

You may think of feedback as the way your teacher corrects or praises you when you're doing exercises or tasks in class. Of course, this is very helpful, but there are many other forms of feedback that can be useful in helping you not only to improve your speaking skills, but also your understanding.

Some studies show that when parents give small children feedback, they don't correct what the children say but rather rephrase it to make what they say more comprehensible or standard. Some adults may do the same when speaking to foreign language learners. It's worth making an effort to listen to the way responses you get in real communication are worded, for example in shops or restaurants. In the early stages, some people may rephrase what you say to make sure they have understood you. This can also provide useful input, such as vocabulary that you can use yourself.

When listening and interacting with others, if you don't understand, ask them to rephrase what they have said. Similarly, if they look confused when you speak, try using other words. Negotiating understanding in this way will help both your understanding and speaking skills.

So it's worth being alert to what others have to say, not just in terms of understanding, but also to learn from them.

Over to you

When you're next speaking to someone in your target language – a tandem partner or your teacher, for example – think about the language they use and how you can pick up useful language from them. If you speak to different people in your target language, reflect on how their language, style or feedback may differ. You might like to note down phrases that you could use yourself when speaking.

You could, for example, aim to note and learn a couple of useful phrases per week and then try to use them next time you speak to someone. Try noting down some phrases that come to mind now.

....

....

....

65 Working with a tandem partner

See Tip 16 *Learn with a tandem partner* if you want to remind yourself about what a tandem partner is.

Here, we look at how you can make the most of working with a tandem partner. For example, it's important that you:

- contribute equally in terms of effort in each meeting
- give equal time to each language
- don't mix the languages, but you speak one language at a time together.

You and your tandem partner decide together what you want to learn and how, so if your aim is to use your target language on holiday, you could discuss holiday destinations together and practise the kind of language you're likely to need when travelling. You could study useful vocabulary before your meeting and then practise using it, for example concerning food or transport. You could also read an article on a topic of mutual interest before you meet and then discuss it. All of this preparation before you meet will help you improve your understanding as well as your speaking skills.

Try to introduce variety into your sessions and find common ground in terms of interests. There are many possible starting points, such as films, newspaper or magazine articles, and short recordings such as travel blogs and TED Talks. You will certainly think of more.

If your partner's level is fairly low, don't be tempted to correct every mistake he or she makes. This can be inhibiting. Instead, focus on understanding the main message and ask questions to clarify meaning. You and your partner can also rephrase or summarise what is said, to make it clearer and reinforce your understanding.

If you aren't able to meet your tandem partner regularly, you may find it useful to email or message each other between sessions. You could use your first languages to give each other extra reading practice or you could take the opportunity to practise writing in your target languages.

If your levels are advanced, you will have had considerable learning experience and may wish to be corrected more frequently, but even if this is the case it's better to identify habitual errors rather than correct every slip and error. It can be helpful to note errors when your partner is speaking and review them at the end of the session. Discuss how you want to correct each other when you first meet.

Over to you

How can you and your tandem partner help each other and benefit from each other in improving your understanding?

Here are some ideas:

Summarise a text or audio/video recording you have read, listened to or watched. Your partner can then ask you questions about the subject. Note down some texts or audio/video recordings that would work well for this.

. . . .

. . . .

. . . .

. . . .

Give your partner a text to read or a listening exercise and ask questions about it to check his or her understanding. Make sure the chosen text or exercise is at a suitable level, neither too difficult nor too easy. Note down some texts or listening exercises that would work well for this.

. . . .

. . . .

. . . .

. . . .

Imagine you are famous people – interview each other. You could role-play the situation with specific celebrities in mind. Who would you like to be?

. . . .

. . . .

Can you think of more ideas for activities with your tandem partner?

. . . .

. . . .

. . . .

. . . .

. . . .

Key points

In this section, we have considered improving understanding of authentic language. Here are some key points to remember:

- Read what you enjoy.
- Read a lot!
- Be aware of why and how you're reading.
- Work on improving vocabulary through extensive and intensive reading.
- Choose listening sources you enjoy.
- Listen to the language as often as possible with very short and longer sessions.
- Be aware of pitfalls in listening and how you can overcome them.
- Vary and adapt your approach as you make progress.
- Take advantage of all opportunities to speak in a variety of contexts.
- Listen carefully to the way the person you're talking to expresses him or herself.
- Be aware of the value of direct and indirect feedback from the people you're speaking to.

My own take-home notes on Improving understanding

G Sounding good

Speak the speech, I pray you, as I pronounced it to you, trippingly on the tongue.

William Shakespeare (1564–1616): *Hamlet*, Act 3 Scene 2

In this section, we focus on the topic of pronunciation, referring to areas such as accent, stress and intonation. We will consider the relationship between identity and pronunciation and will discuss ways in which you can, if you wish to, make yourself sound more like a native speaker.

Aims of this section

The tips in this section show you:

- why it's useful to decide how good you want or need your pronunciation to be
- why your focus should be on making your pronunciation clear and easily intelligible
- ways of using drama activities and singing to improve your pronunciation
- techniques for using poetry to help with your pronunciation
- how to find out about the individual sounds in your target language and the International Phonetic Alphabet (IPA) symbols for them
- ways of becoming more aware of stress and intonation
- why it's important to know about word stress and intonation in your target language.

66 How do you want to sound?

Do you want to sound like a native speaker?

Some speakers can become so good at pronouncing their target language that they can pass themselves off as native speakers. To be able to do so, however, is extremely uncommon. If you don't learn a language in early childhood, it can be hard to hear the difference between sounds that are not differentiated in your own language, let alone pronounce them as a native speaker might. For example, many learners of English find it hard, if not impossible, to differentiate between, say, *cup* and *cap* or *ship* and *sheep*. Similarly, many learners of Russian find it hard to distinguish between the two different 'l' sounds which Russian has (usually referred to as hard and soft 'l'); for example, 'el' means 'ate' when it's pronounced with a hard 'l' and 'fir tree' when it's pronounced with a soft 'l'.

Even if you wanted to speak like a native speaker, there is often a wide range of native speaker accents you could aspire to. English is an extreme example: learners could go for Australian English, British English, Indian English, New Zealand English, Nigerian English or North American English, among others. Supposing they opt for British English, there are then a vast number of local accents to select from. Professor Higgins, the famous phonetics professor in *Pygmalion*, a play by George Bernard Shaw, boasted that he could place any British man within six miles of his home merely by listening to his voice. Of course, other languages have varied pronunciations too; there are, for example, considerable differences between the pronunciations of Austrian German and German from the north of Germany or between Sicilian and Roman Italian.

Pronunciation tends to be strongly bound up with identity. Native speakers are often proud of their local accent and reluctant to lose it even if their teachers may sometimes encourage them to speak with a standard accent. In a similar way, some learners will be reluctant to attempt to speak their target language exactly as a native speaker does, feeling that it would somehow mean losing their own personality. However, getting over such feelings can be an important step on the way to speaking the language confidently and well.

For most people, the main pronunciation aim should be to pronounce the language so they will be understood without any confusion. A leading British newspaper reported how a Japanese tourist in London once wanted to travel on to Turkey (via Heathrow airport). She said she was going to Turkey at a London railway station and expected to be directed to the airport, but she was put on a train to the seaside resort of Torquay. You obviously want to avoid that kind of misunderstanding, but a slight foreign accent in a language won't normally impede communication and may indeed be considered attractive.

So, unless you want to become a spy or a top professor of the language, it makes sense to aim to have good rather than perfect pronunciation. In most cases you should probably go for what is considered standard pronunciation. This is likely to be the dominant accent on television or radio news programmes and it will be the pronunciation exemplified in dictionaries and materials teaching the language. Just remain aware, however, that you may well encounter many speakers who don't pronounce words in exactly the way you expect.

Over to you

On a scale from 1 to 5, where 1 means not at all and 5 very much, how much would you like to sound like a native speaker of your target language? Note down the reasons why you feel this.

....

....

....

....

Are there key differences in pronunciation styles among major varieties of your target language? Ask your teacher or someone who knows your target language well if you're unsure about this.

....

....

....

....

67 Losing your inhibitions

Many people report feeling shy and slightly embarrassed when it comes to speaking a foreign language. Using unfamiliar sounds and intonation patterns may seem odd and unnatural to you. It has been argued that when we speak another language we take on a different personality. To speak a foreign language well, you need to be prepared to let go of your usual self and become someone who is in some ways rather different. Developing performance skills may help you do this. It may seem counter-intuitive but many stars of entertainment are actually quite shy in their private lives. Brad Pitt, Kim Kardashian West, Justin Timberlake, Elton John and Lady Gaga are among the famous stars who are comfortable in front of an audience but who have owned up to being introverted and lacking in self-confidence when not performing. If you find it easy to slip into a new persona, then you may naturally find it easier to speak another language. If you don't, then the techniques here may be particularly useful for you.

Using drama

Drama can help your pronunciation in a number of ways. Not only does pretending to be someone else help to overcome feelings of embarrassment, it also involves having to speak as clearly and meaningfully as possible so an audience will understand and be engaged by your performance. Moreover, it requires plenty of repetition, which is invaluable when it comes to fixing new language in your memory.

You can gain all these benefits by getting together with others to put on a little play in your target language. If you're studying in a language class, perhaps you could ask your teacher to suggest something suitable for your level and the size of your group. It may not be practically possible to do all the rehearsing necessary to put on a full-scale performance with everyone learning all their lines but you could consider making an audio recording of your performance. The process of assigning parts, discussing each person's character and role and reading the play through together as many times as necessary to get to the point where you feel good enough to make the recording will benefit your speaking skills enormously, including your pronunciation. You can then learn even more by listening to the recording and considering how you could improve on it.

If you can't find a group to work with, you might be able to do a little bit of drama on your own. Can you find an audio or video recording of a piece of drama on the internet in your target language, ideally one that you have the script for or can transcribe yourself? Stop the recording at regular points and repeat what the actor has just said, imitating his or her pronunciation as closely as possible. Then try speaking simultaneously with the actor. It's good to do this activity with a piece of drama as actors have to pronounce clearly and with feeling and so are a good model for a learner to copy.

Songs

Singing is also a wonderful tool for language learners. Many of us choose to listen to a recording of our favourite songs over and over again. If we do this with a song in our target language then we will gradually pick up the words of that song until we know it so well that we can sing along with the recording. This is a wonderful way of doing something that is pure enjoyment but also has enormous advantages in terms of our language learning, benefitting our acquisition of vocabulary and grammar as well as our pronunciation.

Some songs are more suitable from the point of view of language learning than others. It's probably better to go for a singer who has clear pronunciation and for songs that are in relatively standard language. If you like the song and find the words have some significance for you personally, then that may also mean your learning is more effective. If you find a song you like, it can then be interesting to look on YouTube for different singers' versions of it. If you can't make out all the words, don't worry as many song lyrics are available on the internet. If you don't know much about singers in your target language, ask your teacher or someone who knows the language well for recommendations. You could also try listening to online radio in your target language until you identify a performer whose style meets your needs.

If you can find a karaoke machine or app with songs in your target language, that is also an ideal way of both improving your pronunciation and having fun with friends.

Over to you

Have you had any experience of participating in drama or singing activities in your own or any other language? If so, how did it make you feel?

....

....

If you live in a country where your target language is spoken, is there an appropriate drama club, choir or other singing group that you could join in your area?

....

....

Have you got access to an app or some other means of doing karaoke in your target language? If not, do some research to see what is available.

....

....

Note down the names of some songs or performers in your target language who you would like to sing along with.

....

....

....

....

....

....

....

....

68 Using poetry

Poetry is an effective and enjoyable way of improving your pronunciation in your target language. Poems are typically characterised by rhyme and rhythm, both of which are significant elements of pronunciation. The traditional importance of poetry is highlighted by the fact that nursery rhymes are part of young children's introduction to the fun that can be had with language.

Some cultures and some periods of history have given greater importance to the learning of poetry by heart than other cultures and periods have. Homer's *Odyssey*, after all, was for many centuries passed on orally from one generation to the next. The rhythm and rhymes that characterise poetry make it more straightforward to learn than a piece of prose would be.

Some people would argue that much poetry is not written in normal everyday language and that it may therefore not provide a good model of what you should be aiming for. It's undoubtedly true that some poems, particularly those from earlier centuries, use vocabulary and expressions that might sound very strange in everyday speech. However, learning poetry can provide you not only with knowledge of the culture of your target language but also with an understanding of how words are stressed and how they rhyme.

Use poetry that appeals to you. You may be someone who is fascinated by the classical poetry of the past or you may feel that modern verse has more relevance for you. You could do a web search for 'best poems in [your target language]'. It's a good idea to base your learning of a poem on a recording read by a native speaker of the language. For 20th and 21st century poetry, you may well be able to find a recording made by the poet him or herself. If you can't find one online, ask a native speaker or someone who speaks the language well to read and record the poem(s) so you can listen again and again and can also practise reading the poem(s) aloud at the same time.

A good place to start might be by learning some verses aimed at schoolchildren as they tend to be in more straightforward language and often make a particularly obvious use of rhyme. They also frequently exploit repetition, which has value for both first and second language learners. The only thing to guard against is any use of the nonsense words that sometimes characterise children's verse, so it makes sense to choose wisely. As usual, ask a teacher or someone who knows the language well for advice if you're unsure where to start.

Over to you

Find a short, contemporary poem in your target language online and write down the words. Then either find or make a recording of someone reading the poem aloud.

....

....

....

....

....

....

....

....

....

....

Do a web search for 'poems for children in [your target language]'. Explore any websites you find. Note the web addresses and save any that you feel might be particularly useful to your Favourites menu.

....

....

....

....

....

....

....

....

....

69 Individual sounds

One of the first things you need to do when learning a new language is to try to get to grips with its individual sounds. The extent to which this might be difficult will depend on how close your own first language is to your target language. A Swede who is learning English will have far fewer problems with regard to pronunciation than a Swede who is learning Mandarin.

There is a system called the International Phonetic Alphabet (IPA) which allows us to write words in any language exactly as they are pronounced. It is based on the Latin alphabet but also uses symbols for additional sounds. Thus the English word *love* would be written as /lʌv/ in IPA. This system is particularly useful for languages in which the spelling of a word doesn't tell you how to pronounce it. English is a prime example of this – compare *bough, cough, tough, dough, through, thorough* and *ought*. The pronunciation of *ough* in each of these words is represented by a different symbol in IPA. The representations of these words in standard British English pronunciation are: /baʊ/, /kɒf/, /tʌf/, /dəʊ/, /θruː/, /ˈθʌrə/ and /ɔːt/.

These are the IPA symbols that are relevant for English:

Vowels

iː see	ɪ sit	ʊ look	uː two	e set	ə ago		
ɜː word	ɔː more	æ sat	ʌ cut	ɑː hard	ɒ lot		
ɪə near	eɪ say	ʊə tour	ɔɪ toy	əʊ so	eə wear	aɪ my	aʊ cow

Consonants

p pot	b buy	t tap	d do	tʃ chip	dʒ edge	k cup	g go
f far	v vet	θ thing	ð the	s so	z zoo	ʃ she	ʒ Asia
m man	n no	ŋ sing	h he	l low	r red	w wet	j you

IPA symbols are often used in print dictionaries to represent how a word is pronounced. Electronic ones often have buttons to click so you can hear as well as see the word. The symbols that are relevant vary from language to language. Many languages, for example, don't have the 'th' sounds characteristic of English. However, they will have other sounds that English lacks. Each language therefore requires its own individual IPA chart.

There is a useful website that provides phonetic transcriptions of a number of languages (https://easypronunciation.com/en/). This site gives you a lot of information about the pronunciation of British and US English, French, Russian, Italian, Spanish, Portuguese, Japanese and Chinese, but not all the content is free.

You will find detailed information about the IPA at: https://en.wikipedia.org/wiki/International_Phonetic_Alphabet. You may or may not wish to familiarise yourself with it; inevitably it's a complex system as it can be applied to any language. If the IPA's systematic and analytical approach to pronunciation appeals to you, it makes sense to focus only on those symbols which relate to your target language.

Being aware of the IPA can be useful in a number of ways. It can draw attention to the way in which certain letters in a word may be pronounced differently when they are in a different position in the word. For instance, the last letter of *Hund* (dog) in German is pronounced more like a 't' than a 'd' /hʊnt/ although when an ending is added to make the plural form, it's pronounced as a 'd' sound /h'ʊndə/.

The IPA can also raise awareness of sounds that are unfamiliar from your own first language and these are the ones that you're most likely to need to focus your pronunciation work on. However, you also need to take care with sounds that you may mistakenly think are the same as those in your own language. The letter 'r', for example, is pronounced very differently in English, French and Italian.

Over to you

Do a web search for 'IPA + [your target language]'. Check out any websites you find. How useful do you think you would find the symbols? If you think it would be useful for you, make a poster illustrating the symbols used for your target language, together with examples of words requiring each of those symbols. Or you might be able to download a poster.

....

....

List the sounds in your target language that you think you will need to practise most. If you're not sure what these are, try doing a web search for, say, 'difficult sounds for English speakers to pronounce in Russian'. Ideally this site will also lead you to some activities that will help you master those problem sounds.

....

....

....

70 Beyond individual sounds

Reading along with a recording

One of the most effective ways to improve your pronunciation is to find a recording of a short text made by a good clear speaker of your target language. You will also need a transcript of the text. First listen to the recording several times. Then practise reading it aloud yourself. The most important step is then to read the text aloud along with the recording, i.e. sync your reading with the recording. Doing this will help you to stress words and phrases in an appropriate way and to match the intonation patterns of the speaker.

Stress

When it comes to developing good comprehensible pronunciation, stress and intonation are arguably more important than the accurate pronunciation of individual sounds. The particular issues that you may have with stress and intonation will vary depending on your own first language and your target language.

One basic contrast in pronunciation that is sometimes made between languages is that some languages give much more importance to word stress than others. In some languages, such as French and Spanish, each syllable is given equal weight. In English, on the other hand, stressed syllables are given much more prominence than unstressed ones; notice how differently these words are pronounced – PHOtograph, phoTOGrapher, photoGRAPHical (the stressed syllable in each case is in capitals). Word stress is important in many other languages, including Russian, Arabic and German. Where the stress falls depends on the language. In most long words in Polish, for example, it falls on the penultimate syllable. However, in other languages, there is much more variation in the position of stress in a word.

In languages where word stress is important, you will need to notice which syllable the stress falls on in a longer word and how this affects the pronunciation of the other syllables in that word. Putting the stress on the wrong syllable can sometimes make what you're trying to say surprisingly difficult for others to understand. If your target language is English or Russian, say, and your own first language stresses each syllable in a long word in much the same way, then you will need to make sure you don't give too much weight to the unstressed syllables in a word as that may make your pronunciation hard to understand.

Intonation

Intonation means making your voice rise or fall in order to convey meaning or attitude. Paying attention to the punctuation, say aloud:

Your sister speaks Japanese.
Your sister speaks Japanese?

In the statement, your voice probably fell at the end of the sentence. In the question, it should have risen at the end in order to let the listener know that you were asking a question rather than making a statement.

Different languages use intonation in different ways. Some languages, Chinese, for example, are called tone languages. They make use of rising and falling intonations (or tones) within a word in a way that produces words with completely different meanings. Learning how to understand and use tones will be an important task for you if your target language is tonal.

Some languages tend to be much flatter than others in terms of intonation. English tends to go up and down quite a lot and someone who speaks English with a very flat intonation can sound dull or even rude. It's important to learn about the intonation patterns of your target language so that you come across in the way you wish when you speak.

Over to you

How important is word stress in your target language?

....

Are there rules determining where word stress falls in your target language? Write down 20 to 30 words of differing lengths but all with more than one syllable. Mark where the stress falls on all these words. Most good dictionaries indicate where the word stress falls, so you can check if you aren't sure. Do you notice any particular patterns? If you do, check with your teacher or someone who knows the language well to see if the conclusions you drew were correct.

....

....

....

....

....

Where could you find suitable recordings to read along with, as described in the activity above? Note down some ideas.

....

....

....

....

....

Find a recording to read along to. Try to stress the words and phrases in an appropriate way and to match the intonation patterns of the speaker. Note down any words and phrases that you find particularly difficult.

....

....

....

....

....

....

....

....

Key points

In this section, we have considered ways of improving your pronunciation and sounding good. Here are some key points to remember:

- Your focus should be on making your pronunciation clear and easily intelligible.
- You need to master not only the individual sounds of your target language but also its stress and intonation patterns.
- Drama, songs and poetry all have a valuable role to play in helping you develop good pronunciation.
- Drama, songs and poetry are particularly suitable because they often provide a good model to imitate. They also lend themselves to frequent repetition and are a fun way of improving your pronunciation.

My own take-home notes on Sounding good

H Progressing and making learning stick

Per ardua ad alta.

Through efforts to great heights.

Birmingham University motto

In this section, we look at ways you can take stock of your progress and ensure that you keep at it. But there may be times when you feel you're not progressing. Typically, as beginners, people often make fast progress, but as they move on to an intermediate level they may hit a plateau. But there is no need to get permanently stuck. So the tips in this section give ideas on ways to spice up your learning and explore new ways of approaching learning to help you maintain your motivation and make you stick at it.

Aims of this section

The tips in this section show you:

- why it's helpful to have an overview of different language levels and to gauge your current level
- ways of making the language stick in your brain so it becomes automatic
- techniques for making language stand out so it becomes easier to remember
- how it helps to keep practising until you can use language elements effortlessly
- different ways of boosting your motivation
- the benefits of teaching someone else who is learning your target language
- how to organise your learning around a project
- techniques for building learning practice into your daily life
- ways of practising writing which will consolidate your learning
- why taking a short break from regular language learning isn't necessarily a bad thing
- why it can be helpful to take a test or an official examination.

71 Getting an overview of progress

Language learning isn't linear. If it were, it would be easy to study for a number of weeks or months and see regular progress. In reality, we seem to learn in fits and starts. The brain needs time to assimilate new knowledge and takes this in as and when it appears 'ready', so long as we continue to provide regular input and practice. We may feel frustrated at times as we don't seem to be progressing or, on the other hand, we may be surprised that suddenly we find particular grammar rules easier to understand or realise our listening comprehension is much better. To maintain your motivation and get an idea of the progress you've made, it helps to take stock using a system that categorises language levels and learners' skills.

The Common European Framework of Reference (CEFR) was developed by the Council of Europe. It is used in many countries within and outside Europe and provides a helpful overview of what learners can do at different language learning levels. It can be applied to any language. The chart below draws on the CEFR.

Basic User (beginner)	A1	You can understand and use familiar everyday expressions and very basic phrases to satisfy concrete needs such as introducing yourself and asking and answering questions, for example on where you live.
Basic User (post-beginner / elementary)	A2	You can understand frequently used expressions regarding areas such as family information or shopping. You can communicate on routine tasks with simple and direct language and give information on your background or immediate needs.
Independent User (lower-intermediate)	B1	You can understand the main points concerning familiar matters at school, work or during leisure. You can deal with or get by in most situations when travelling and can talk or write about topics of interest, for example describing experiences and giving opinions.
Independent User (intermediate to upper-intermediate)	B2	You can understand the main ideas of complex language including technical discussions in your field. You can speak fluently and interact easily with speakers of the target language, covering a wide range of subjects, particularly as you reach the higher end of this level.
Proficient User (advanced)	C1	You can understand a wide range of demanding texts including understanding indirect meanings. You can speak fluently with little effort in social, academic or professional settings. You're able to structure your ideas clearly.
Proficient User (very advanced)	C2	You can easily understand almost everything you read or hear and express yourself both very fluently and precisely. You're able to express and understand finer shades of meaning, even in more complex situations.

https://rm.coe.int/cefr-companion-volume-with-new-descriptors-2018/1680787989

It's worth noting that the bands are very broad and it takes time to progress within a band. So you don't necessarily move automatically from B1 to B2, for example, when following a course. You are more likely to move from the beginning of one band to the middle of the same band, and so on.

Over to you

Consider your current ability in relation to your aims and the levels described here. It might be an idea to discuss this with your teacher if you're taking a class.

What level do you think you are at the moment? ....

What level do you hope to be at in, say, six months or a year? ....

Are your aims realistic given the time and support you have? ....

Taking stock from time to time is important, so you may wish to think about your aims in relation to your progress to date and the next steps.

Do you need to set new aims? Or can you carry on as before? ....

If you need to set new aims, what should they be?

....

....

....

....

....

....

Also review your approach to learning and the materials or resources you're using. Would it be helpful to change any of these? If so, how?

....

....

....

....

....

....

Take time to reflect on these points and discuss them with your teacher if you wish.

72 Processing and automatising language

If we give our brains regular access to the language through reading and listening, and opportunities to process, manipulate and use it, for example through writing, speaking or doing vocabulary or grammar exercises, we are more likely to create new links in our brains and anchor the knowledge in our long-term memories.

Psychologists speak of 'deep processing' being particularly effective for any kind of learning. In terms of language learning, this means manipulating the language in a range of ways. For example, when learning vocabulary, this could involve doing vocabulary exercises such as putting new words in context, but then going beyond this in different ways. You could, for example, relate the new words to your personal experience and then tell or write a short story using the words. In processing new language in multiple meaningful ways, you help it to stick.

As the brain takes in new information, particularly with regard to grammar, it takes time to integrate this. Initially, we may not understand a grammar rule, but if we persevere, we find that we begin to understand the point in question. We may need to think about it when we first actively use a new grammar point, but after a while, we begin to use it without thinking. At this stage, the knowledge has become automatic. This is similar to when we learn to drive a car, which can seem complicated when we begin, but becomes relatively effortless over time.

One word of warning though! It's important to consider grammar rules carefully if you want to speak and write the language in its standard form, as it's described in traditional grammar books. It's quite easy just to understand and make yourself understood in many situations without worrying too much about standard forms. This may not be a problem, depending on the contexts in which you intend to use the language and your own aims. But, if you need to use the language in your job or for study, don't skip the analytical work. If you do, you may automatise non-standard forms, but this won't help you to pass an exam or make yourself understood on complex matters.

Here's an example of an exercise you could do as a form of deep processing:

> Photocopy a page of text you have read in your target language. Block out the words you have been memorising and see if you can fill in the gaps the next day. You could do this several times with the same text, blocking out key words you need to know on a particular theme. Or you could block out, say, every tenth word in a text to see what words you need to focus on in terms of vocabulary, depending on how easily you can bring them to mind, or not!

Over to you

Think about your current knowledge of your target language. What can you already do automatically? This might be answering questions on where you live and about your family, or it might be speaking spontaneously about a technical aspect of your job.

....

....

....

....

....

....

Consider what kind of learning activities you have done that might qualify as 'deep processing'. Make a note of them, reflect on them and experiment with different ways of practising new language that will help consolidate and automatise what you have learnt.

....

....

....

....

....

....

73 Taking stock and making difficult points stand out

You may find some points just don't stick, which can be frustrating of course. These may be words you can't remember or grammar rules you can't seem to master or apply correctly. On the one hand, it's important to remember that language learning takes time and that you may simply need to allow more time for the points concerned to stick. You might also be setting the bar too high and need to go back to easier tasks for a while.

If you find you have sticking points, it can be helpful to pay particular attention to them. You can make important points **stand out** so that your brain focuses particularly on them and is thus more likely to assimilate them. This doesn't need to be hard work.

For example, if you're learning words relating to the human body, you could:

- Copy/photocopy or download a picture showing different parts of the body. As mentioned in Tip 39 *Connecting words with concepts*, visual materials for basic vocabulary are often designed for children learning their mother tongue, and these can also be useful for adults learning that language as they aren't too complex. You may find it helpful to highlight or underline the words you're finding it difficult to remember.
- Focus on these words every morning and evening; cover them up and test yourself.
- When you begin to find the words easier to remember, integrate them into a short text, highlighting or underlining them. One way of helping to fix the words in your mind would be to relate the text to yourself, telling a story or describing yourself. You could also make up a memorable, imaginary text. Here is an example, but more important than this example is finding something that is memorable to you:

> I love travelling and sometimes dream I'm on my travels. Recently, I dreamt that I was in a desert on a camel. Suddenly, I came across an enormous statue of a man that had fallen to the ground and was broken. His head had fallen off his body. You could still see his face though, with a broad forehead, big eyes, a long nose, smiling mouth and big ears. One of his arms was broken above the wrist and the second below the shoulder and above the elbow. Some fingers and one thumb seemed to be missing. The man's chest was broad and

> his waist slim. He had a cloth over his hips. Surprisingly, his legs were not broken. The cloth covered his thighs and knees. His calves (grammar note: calf singular) were strong and he had sandals on his feet (grammar note: foot singular) and over his ankles. His toes were broken.

- You could do a drawing to accompany your text.
- After a while, you should be able to visualise the statue and recall the text from memory without reading it. This will also help to fix the words in your long-term memory.

Over to you

Do you have something you're finding it difficult to memorise? Design an exercise to overcome the problem. You can draw on the ideas above or invent your own.

....

....

....

....

....

....

Remember to break the task down into several phases. Make key points stand out and allow lots of time to work on the task, monitoring how you get on.

74 Overlearning

Another concept that has been shown to produce long-term results is overlearning. This might sound as if it's something negative like overeating or oversleeping but it's actually something that is beneficial. It means going over and over the elements you need to know until you can use them effortlessly.

Below is an example showing how you can focus on prepositions in German. Prepositions tend to be difficult in most languages as their use frequently seems arbitrary. In German, prepositions affect the words that follow them. Some prepositions need to be followed by one case and some by another. Nouns have four cases in German (nominative, accusative, dative and genitive) and changing the case involves making slight changes to the ending of the basic word. When articles and adjectives are involved their endings may change too.

- Focus on reasonably simple elements. We have drawn up a list of prepositions that are followed by the accusative in German (other prepositions are followed by different cases). Having a sentence that shows the meaning in context is important so you know how to use the word. Also highlight or underline the key points, in this case the different forms of prepositions.
- Initially, memorise the list of prepositions – learn them by heart until you can recite them easily. This may take several practice sessions. Review the example sentences, which you can personalise; this will also help fix the prepositions in your mind. Keep going over them, for example before you go to sleep, even when you think you know them. Then try to notice and use them when you're working on the language.

+ Accusative		
durch	through	Die neue Autobahn verläuft direkt **durch eine** Urlaubsregion. The new motorway runs directly through a holiday area.
für	for	**Für dich** würde ich alles tun! I'd do anything for you!
gegen	against	Ich brauche etwas **gegen die** Grippe. I need something for flu.
ohne	without	**Ohne meine** Brille sehe ich nichts. I can't see anything without my glasses.
um	around	Sie trägt immer hübsche Tücher **um den** Hals. She always wears pretty scarves around her neck.

Over to you

What aspect of your target language could you focus on to improve your memory by overlearning?

. . . .

. . . .

Design a simple activity to do this and fit it into your daily schedule.

. . . .

. . . .

. . . .

. . . .

. . . .

. . . .

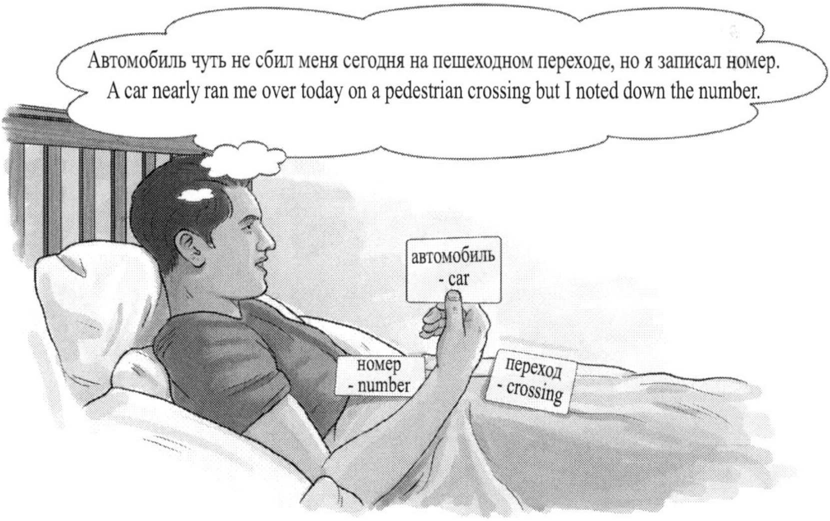

75 Maintaining motivation

Keeping up your motivation is essential if you're to reach your language learning aims. So it's worth getting hooked on activities in the target language that will boost your motivation and help you to continue progressing. Some ideas are given in this tip and also explored in Sections B, D and G.

Become an online gamer. It doesn't matter how young or old you are, online gaming offers something for everyone and is a good way to use the language in communicating with others, focusing on language use rather than learning. But, of course, you will also learn as real communication will help you to progress.

Become a news junkie. Sign up for news apps from a range of media. You can just listen to their reports for information or focus on the way different media report on the same stories, for example, taking different political stances or viewpoints. Some news stories are as brief as one minute and are sometimes available with subtitles. They also offer links to print and audio/video news. If you get hooked to good media sources you will not only immerse yourself in the language, but also be well informed about what is happening in the world.

Watch drama series. With some broadcasting companies, for example the BBC and companies such as Netflix and Amazon Prime, you can watch excellent drama series, ranging from period drama to crime and spy stories. It's easy to become addicted to these!

Find a model speaker. Find someone who speaks your target language well and is someone you would like to sound like. Choose someone appropriate – if you're a teenager, you may not want to sound like someone who is 90, or vice versa. The person that you feel could be a good 'model' may be your teacher or tandem partner or perhaps an actor in a film. You may also come across specialists in different fields who can be useful models as they often give talks, make podcasts and appear in the media. Listen to them as often as possible, noting down useful phrases you could use and getting a feeling for their rhythm and tone. Their style may be humorous, precise, formal or informal, depending on the model you choose. By immersing yourself in their language you will also begin to understand more, for example idioms that may be similar to idioms you use in your own language. It's also a fairly effortless way of staying motivated and making progress!

Over to you

Consider the suggestions above and choose one that suits your schedule and interests. Note down your ideas and give it a try!

....

....

....

....

....

....

Maybe you're already doing one or more of the activities here or perhaps you have other ideas. The main point is to try something new that is really motivating and will be such fun that you will want to do it over and over again.

76 Teach someone else

The Roman philosopher Seneca is said to have recognised that we learn when teaching others, saying that 'men [*sic*] learn when they teach'. More recently, studies have indeed shown that we ourselves can benefit by passing on our knowledge to others.

You may have chosen to study your target language because one of your children is studying the language. If so, you can work on the homework together, test each other on the vocabulary and find other interesting activities to do together. If you learnt the language at school and are rusty, this gives you a head start and you can brush up your knowledge to run over key points with your child.

At intermediate or advanced levels, you may find a beginner or lower-level student to help, either from another class if you're taking a course, or by putting a notice on a school or library noticeboard.

Teaching someone else is of value for a number of reasons:

- In preparing to teach, you need to remember and clarify key points in your own mind. This will show you how well you understand these points, or not ...
- In teaching another person, you have to review the material you intend to teach, go over it and practise explaining it clearly (all well-trained teachers do this!).
- By going over the points again with another person, you are, in fact, drawing on deep processing, which will help to consolidate and automatise this knowledge even more.
- When you teach, the feedback you get will show how well you have done. You may also be asked questions that you can either answer easily or need to research and answer later.

If you like teaching, this could be an ideal opportunity for you. If not, why not give it a try; you might find it useful and surprisingly enjoyable. But only work with learners at an appropriate level – you shouldn't present yourself as a professional language teacher if you're still in the early stages of learning the language yourself!

Over to you

If you would like to try teaching someone else some aspects of your target language that you have already studied and feel confident about, consider these questions:

Who could I teach?

....

....

Where can I find this person?

....

....

What aspects of the language could I teach them? (this will also depend on the person's needs)

....

....

....

....

....

....

77 Practise, practise, practise

One of the best ways to progress and consolidate your learning is to practise as much as possible. Practice should be varied and, of course, interesting and motivating.

An interesting approach to practice that has proved effective in language learning is to organise your learning around a project. The project doesn't need to concern something you intend to do in real life, although of course it could do, but it should be based on a subject you find really interesting.

Here are a couple of examples of the kind of project that would give you a lot of practice using the language and encourage you to work on it regularly.

Mini-research project

Focus your practice on a subject that interests you, such as one of the following:

- a holiday in one of the countries where your target language is spoken
- how to lose weight or get fit
- a prospective pet, e.g. a cat, dog or donkey
- ways for elderly people to have more social contact.

First, in the target language, do some online or paper-based research on your chosen subject. Draw up a 'to do' list to identify and tick off each point that you cover. Don't be overambitious, spread the project out over at least a month, working on it a couple of days a week, for example. Your research will involve reading and listening and perhaps speaking and writing. You could, for example, interview someone on the subject, preparing your questions in writing beforehand. You could also summarise and discuss your findings with your classmates or tandem partner, or on online forums, or write a report for your teacher.

Skills-focused project

Another way of getting practice could be to focus on one skill or aspect of language learning each day of the week with one day off, as illustrated in the following table. After completing one week you can either work more on the same subject or start a new subject. You might like to do this from time to time, for example during the college holidays if you're taking a course.

Day	Skill	Time	Source and focus
Monday	Vocabulary	15 mins	Find and note vocabulary on a particular theme, e.g. the environment.
Tuesday	Reading	20 mins	Read a short article on the subject. See how many words you recognise and note others you want to learn.
Wednesday	Listening	20 mins	Listen to a short audio or video recording on the same subject. Listen more than once, focusing on the key ideas or details, depending on your level.
Thursday	Speaking	10 mins	Summarise the key ideas in the target language, either just for yourself or by leading this into a conversation with someone else.
Friday	Grammar	10 mins	Look back at the article and highlight or underline grammar points that you have already covered but may need to do more work on.
Saturday	Writing	15 mins	Recycle the words you have learnt into a short text.
Sunday	Day off!		

Over to you

Would you like to test out one of the suggestions above? How would you modify the suggestions to suit your individual needs and interests? You could fill in the chart below to suit your needs.

Day	Skill	Time	Source and focus
Monday			
Tuesday			
Wednesday			
Thursday			
Friday			
Saturday			
Sunday			

78 Write to consolidate and extend your knowledge

Writing can be frustrating in the early stages of learning as what you write may not make your meaning clear if you're writing an email, for example, or may be returned with a lot of red ink if you're writing in a class context.

Nevertheless, as you improve, writing offers a very effective and stimulating way of progressing in the language. Ideally, you should write something meaningful that your reader needs to read and will respond to. This could be a WhatsApp message to your tandem partner arranging or postponing your next meeting. The responses you receive will also give you helpful phrases that you can copy and use.

As you progress, there is a range of text types you can write either by hand or digitally. You could, for example, write feedback to the manager of a place you have recently visited or a hotel you have stayed in; this could just be an exercise, you don't need to send it. You can give online feedback on products you have bought or ask for advice on forums about products you're interested in buying or places you wish to visit. Such writing can be very brief or longer if you prefer.

If you read a newspaper in your target language, what about writing a letter or email to the editor either in response to an article or simply to say how much you enjoy reading the paper and how it is helping you to learn the language. Before sending a letter or email, it would be a good idea to ask your teacher or tandem partner to review it with you.

You can also write a summary of an article you have read and review this with your teacher or tandem partner. This might be very short at a lower level, or more ambitious both in terms of the length and complexity of the article and the summary at an advanced level.

If you like writing a diary, you may simply wish to write for yourself. This could be as short as one line a day in the target language initially, getting longer as you progress. Reviewing what you have written over time can also show you how you're progressing.

Over to you

Who can you write to in your target language?

....

....

....

....

What can you write to them? Perhaps an invitation to go to the cinema. After that, you could write a message to someone else recommending a film you have seen and saying why you enjoyed it.

....

....

....

....

Who else could you write to?

....

....

....

....

Choose two types of text and practise writing them. Make sure your writing is enjoyable and fits into your daily or weekly schedule.

....

....

....

....

....

....

....

....

79 Take a break

If you have worked regularly on your target language, but feel you need a break, this may not be a bad thing.

A break may come naturally if you're taking a course and the term or semester ends. You may decide not to work on the language at all for a couple of weeks, or simply to lighten the load by focusing on listening or reading, for example, but not working on vocabulary, grammar, speaking and writing.

If you do stop altogether, ensure that you make a date with yourself beforehand for the day you intend to start again. Also write a brief 'to do' list of what you will start working on, then make sure that you have the materials ready in advance. If you don't want to stop completely or have to cut back because of unexpected personal or professional commitments, just schedule a couple of short activities per week such as viewing interesting short videos on YouTube or listening to a podcast.

When you stop working actively on the language, this can give your brain time to reorganise the new knowledge you have been working on. After the break, you should have renewed enthusiasm to get back to regular learning.

Over to you

Do you feel you need to take a break from language learning? The reasons may be clear, but if you're not sure, consider why a break might or might not be a good idea.

Then answer the following questions:

How long should the break be? ....

Will it be a complete break or just lightening your language learning load?

....

How can you organise your time and focus if you want to work on the language a couple of times per week with easy and enjoyable activities?

....

For a complete break, what should you focus on when you start again?

....

80 Test yourself

There's no doubt that testing focuses the mind. For many languages, there are official language testing services. These tests or exams can be expensive to enter but may be required for your job or to enhance your recruitment chances. Even if you don't need an official certificate, you may find it motivating to sign up for an exam preparation course in your target language. Choose your college or school carefully and find out how many of their students take official exams each year and what their pass rate is.

Exam courses are best if they are based on a book designed to meet the level of the exam. This way, you have a systematic approach, working gradually towards the level of the exam and covering all aspects of the language. Simply working on past tests or with test books does not provide this systematic approach. It can, though, be helpful alongside the main coursebook as you approach the exam. Listen to your teacher's advice. If he or she doesn't feel you're ready for the exam, you can take it at the next session. Passing an exam certainly boosts confidence, failing doesn't!

If you do decide to study for an official test, choose an examining board that is widely recognised, for example by employers. For European languages, many examining boards align their examinations with the CEFR levels. This is, for example, the case with DELE *Diplomas de Español como Lengua Extranjera*, which is administered by the Instituto Cervantes for the Spanish Ministry of Education and Science.

You can often study for official tests and examinations in your home country, but if you have the time and funds, you could spend a period of time studying in a country where your target language is spoken. Again, choose the college or school carefully and make sure they have an appropriate entry test and provide advice to ensure that the exam courses they offer are suitable for you.

If you don't like exams, don't have the time or don't want to take a course, you can still borrow or buy test books that you can use to measure your progress and give yourself insights into your strengths and weaknesses, for example in reading or listening. Many examining boards also offer free online testing exercises you can access. If you work with such materials, use them as complements to your overall approach to language learning. Do the tests from time to time, but don't overuse them. Their purpose is to test and not teach, so while they can help you measure your progress and show you what to spend more time on, they don't provide specific learning input.

Over to you

Do you want to take an official examination? Yes / No

If yes, what examinations are there in your target language?

....

....

....

....

....

What examination interests you and where can you get information about it?

....

....

Where could you take a course for the examination?

....

....

Where can you borrow, buy or access testing materials to work on independently?

....

....

What are your next steps?

....

....

....

....

....

Key points

In this section, we have considered ways of taking stock of your progress and making learning stick. Here are some key points to remember:

- It is very important to take stock and have an overview of language levels.
- There are different ways of making language learning stick in the long term, for example through deep processing and overlearning.
- It's helpful to make difficult points **stand out** and to explore ways of working on them.
- Try out fun ways to stay motivated, for example by becoming a news junkie or online gamer.
- Teaching someone else can help you to progress.
- Practice is essential; try out varied and stimulating ways of practising, such as working on a project.
- Writing is helpful; experiment with different ways of making writing support your language learning.
- Taking a break can do you good, so long as you have a plan to start again afterwards!
- Think about the pros and cons of taking tests and examinations.

My own take-home notes on Progressing and making learning stick

....

....

....

....

....

....

....

....

....

I Communicating in different cultures

The world is a book and those who do not travel read only one page.
Saint Augustine of Hippo (354–430)

In this section, we focus on intercultural communication. We include verbal interactions both in speech and writing, and non-verbal interactions between people from different cultural backgrounds. There are numerous books written on intercultural communication, courses to take and research studies carried out on the subject. Here, we give you pointers to a few aspects of the topic that will help you to enjoy the intercultural experience when you begin using your language skills in different contexts.

Aims of this section

The tips in this section aim to show you:

- why it's helpful to consider what is appropriate in a particular context
- how grammatical differences are related to politeness in some languages
- how different cultures vary in their approach to such things as building relationships and achieving goals
- how some cultures communicate in a direct way and others favour more indirect communication
- why some people can experience culture shock and the dangers of stereotyping
- how conventions such as greeting people and gift-giving vary between cultures
- how non-verbal behaviour varies in different cultures and why it's important to be aware of differences
- why awareness of cultural differences and adapting your language and behaviour are important
- how to build techniques for using social talk into your learning practice
- how humour can be a helpful tool when speaking a foreign language
- how to find someone from your target culture who can help you learn about the culture
- how languages function when used as lingua francas.

81 Politeness

Part of the fun of speaking a foreign language involves discovering different cultures. However, there can be challenges. Just as many intercultural encounters can be fascinating, there can also be misunderstandings and we may inadvertently offend others. Such problems can be related to notions of politeness. For example, it may be perfectly normal and considered polite in one culture to kiss or shake hands with others in social or even professional contexts, whereas in other cultures this could be offensive.

One would like to think that most people consider themselves polite. But many people don't realise that although politeness is a universal concept, without which societies would not function at least reasonably smoothly, the way politeness is enacted differs from one culture to another.

Politeness is based on social norms; put simply, politeness within particular cultures is what has developed to be 'normal' and thus automatic. We learn the 'rules' as children and each family or social group may have variants of particular social norms. It can be helpful to consider what is *appropriate* in a particular context rather than polite, to avoid personal or moral judgements.

In any culture, what is appropriate in one context may not be appropriate in another. For example, in most cultures one would not behave the same way in a street market as one would in a court of law. But when you move to or travel through a new culture, you may need to reassess what is appropriate, even in simple contexts such as in shops, at bus stops or in self-service restaurants. If you do what is 'normal' for you, but this is not appropriate in your new context, you may appear impolite or confuse the people you're dealing with. And you may not get what you want!

How can you avoid potential problems? One way is to keep your eyes and ears open. Watch what local people do in all the social situations you find yourself in. Also be aware of their reactions to you. If you're not sure what to say or how to behave, ask! If you think you may have offended someone, explain that you're learning the language and apologise. Also, beware of being so focused on what you're trying to do or achieve that you fail to notice or hear friendly greetings or goodbyes. No one likes to be ignored!

In some situations, such as when there are epidemics or pandemics, people's cultural behaviours change. The Covid-19 pandemic, for example, made people all around the world move further apart from one another in public places than had previously been the case.

Over to you

If you're in a country where your target language is spoken, do some observation. For example, how do people greet salespeople and ask for service in shops? Does this differ from what you would typically say or do?

....

....

....

....

If you don't have direct access to a context where your target language is spoken, try to watch some television programmes or films that can give you insights into how people behave in different everyday contexts when using your target language.

Note down some useful TV programmes or films and make notes on anything you notice when you watch them.

....

....

....

....

....

82 Grammar and politeness

Some languages have grammatical forms that are used to express respect or closeness. For example, many European languages have different pronouns and verb forms such as *tu/vous* in French, *du/Sie* in German and *ty/vy* in Russian, all meaning *you*. Using the forms correctly requires a knowledge of the language and cultural norms when speaking to people you don't know.

In French, a parent asking a child about his or her day at school would say: *As-tu passé une bonne journée?* (Did you have a nice day?), whereas when speaking to the child's teacher he or she would probably use 'vous' (*Avez-vous passé une bonne journée?*), unless the teacher is a family friend. Children learn to use these forms as they grow up, but it's difficult for outsiders to understand the subtleties of use if their native languages don't have such differences. Also, so-called rules often don't reflect reality. If you're unsure, it's safest to stick to the formal form, but even safer to ask how people expect to be addressed. Within cultures and across cultures using the same languages there may also be differences depending on the context, for example social or professional.

Similarly, honorifics are an integral part of languages such as Japanese or Korean. Honorifics are grammatical or lexical additions, such as titles, that express respect to the addressee. In Japanese, they are often expressed through suffixes which relate to respect for hierarchical differences, relational intimacy and humility. Such systems are complex for outsiders, yet it's important to have an idea of how they work, to avoid offence. One of the best ways to learn appropriate use, apart from a grammar book, is by having a cultural insider or guide, which we discuss in Tip 89 *Cultural guides.*

Over to you

Consult the following website and see what it has to say about honorifics in your target language: https://en.wikipedia.org/wiki/Honorific/. You may like to make some notes.

....

Ask your teacher, tandem partner or someone from your target language culture or cultures what politeness rules children are taught when learning to speak the language. Are they similar to or different from politeness rules in your own language and culture?

....

83 Communication and cultural differences

Here we consider some aspects of communication that can differ considerably both individually and across cultures and that can thus potentially cause misunderstanding or offence.

Relationships first – or goals …

When we are at work, our talk tends to be largely oriented towards achieving goals, while in the family and with friends we may focus more on building and nurturing relationships. However, both aspects of communication are present at least to some extent in all contexts. There are, of course, individual differences; some people will take more time chatting in business contexts before discussing business, while others want to get on with the job at once! This also varies from one culture to another. Often in Asian countries, building relationships is considered a priority in business, with considerable time given to this before getting down to work. On the other hand, in North America, a direct approach to business is more common, with very brief small talk before focusing on business.

Directness

There are also both individual and cultural differences in terms of how direct or indirect people are when they communicate. Just as some individuals may wish to get straight down to business and forgo getting to know their partners, there are also differences in how direct or indirect people are in the way they communicate. This is also reflected in cultural differences. Some Asian cultures are often considered to be less direct than Europeans or North Americans, tending to hint at what they wish to convey as a way of showing respect and to avoid conflict. Problems can arise if neither party realises it is operating on a different system. One party may naturally be very explicit and get straight to the point, potentially appearing brusque and perceived to be showing little respect, while the other's indirect style may make them seem evasive to their partners. Discussing such differences can help, as can adapting to each other and meeting on middle ground.

It's helpful to think about the way you communicate as an individual. When communicating in cultures that are different from yours, you can pay attention to whether messages are direct and explicit or indirect. You can then adapt your communication. For example, you may need to be prepared to allow more time to understand implicit messages and to build relationships and common understanding. Even a simple smile may be misinterpreted. In some contexts, failing to smile may be considered rude, while in others doing so may seem inappropriate, perhaps not serious enough. In some cultures, smiling may also convey that the person is ill at ease.

Silence and overlap

Cultures also vary in the extent to which they tolerate silence. People in some cultures tend to find silences in a conversation threatening whereas in others silences feel comfortable and are easily tolerated. Similarly, in some cultures people are more inclined to overlap or speak over one another rather than wait until the previous speaker comes to a close or pauses. At times this may seem inappropriate, but it may be simply an expression of enthusiasm. Tolerance of silence and overlapping when speaking may also vary between individuals. Being aware of potential issues like these will make it much easier for you to accept and adapt to cultural and individual differences.

Over to you

Have you ever been struck by cultural differences in the way people interact in social or professional settings outside your home culture? If possible, think of a specific situation you witnessed in person or perhaps saw in a film.

What differences contrasted with your home culture?

....

....

....

....

To what extent do you think these differences are typical of a particular culture, rather than being determined by the individual communication styles of the people involved, or are they a mixture of both?

....

....

....

....

84 Culture shock

When travelling in another culture for a limited period of time, or moving to another country, some people suffer culture shock. The way of life and living conditions may be very different from their home culture or different from their expectations. The word *shock* tends to have negative connotations; a clash of cultures may make people feel ill at ease or even negative towards the people and the new environment. This may lead to stereotyping.

Stereotyping is often based on generalisations and preconceptions, and is misleading, although an easy trap to fall into. It can occur when negative experiences with individuals lead us to consider the individuals to be representative of the culture as a whole. If you meet people who seem to be impolite, unfriendly or even aggressive, it's worth remembering that such people exist everywhere. There may also be considerable cultural and linguistic differences within one country, so it would also be a generalisation to lump all people from such countries together. Countries such as Switzerland and Nigeria are examples, with different official languages and intercultural differences within the nations. So speaking of 'the Swiss' or 'the Nigerians' is also likely to be misleading.

However, not everyone suffers from culture shock. If you have fallen in love with the language, you may also have read a lot about the culture, so you will be better prepared for cultural differences and able to adapt relatively easily. But some people are so enthusiastic about a new culture that they only see positive aspects of it, going through a 'honeymoon' phase, much like people who have just fallen in love. They may well wake up later to less positive aspects of local reality, but one would hope they won't fall out of love with the language and culture!

You may encounter major cultural differences when you travel or move to another country, but if you can recognise and accept differences, you can adapt to them. Of course, there are also likely to be similarities and areas of common ground to build on.

Finally, studies have shown that people who are open-minded, flexible and, interestingly, who have foreign language skills, are more likely to adapt well to new cultures. Being within the culture of your target language offers wonderful opportunities not only for linguistic immersion, but also to find out about the culture first-hand, to learn culturally appropriate behaviour and accept differences. In this way, you're less likely to suffer culture shock or find yourself in awkward situations.

Over to you

Choose a country you would like to visit or even move to, where your target language is spoken.

Use online resources to do some research on some aspects of everyday life such as:

- education
- food
- housing
- punctuality
- national sports
- shopping
- the economy.

Choose one or two to start with and consider how these are similar or different to your home culture. In what way(s) do you think you might have to adapt to and accept cultural differences?

....

....

....

....

....

....

....

....

....

....

....

....

....

....

85 Rituals and cultural conventions

In all cultures, and within social and professional groups, there are likely to be ritual behaviours based on local cultural conventions. Below are some examples of the kind of ritual behaviours and cultural conventions that differ from one culture to another. To fit in, it's good to be aware of these. It's also worth bearing in mind that within a culture there may be regional differences and generational variations. In addition, habits do change over time.

Meeting and greeting people

Meeting and greeting people can vary from one culture to another. One can fall into the trap of using one's own conventions concerning how to address people, for example, which may cause problems. Many, but far from all, westerners are inclined to use first names these days. Yet in some Asian cultures, first names may be generally used only by family and close friends. Addressing someone by their first name may cause unease or offence in such cases. There may also be generational differences in the way people address each other. If in doubt, ask how you should address the people you're speaking to.

Giving and accepting gifts

When invited to someone's home it's common in most countries to take a gift. Although hosts often say their guests shouldn't have brought anything, they happily accept the gift and it would be unusual to visit empty-handed. Similarly, in many countries, gift-giving is important when doing business. It's a good idea to find out what gifts are appropriate in different cultural contexts. For example, gifts such as fresh flowers are generally welcome, but the choice or even number of flowers may be important. In some cultures, particular flowers can be associated with death – chrysanthemums in France, for example. In Russia, guests must bring an odd number of flowers; an even number is considered bad luck.

Entering people's houses

In many countries around the world it's common to remove one's shoes when entering a private house. This may be for practical reasons. In Canada or Russia it is generally expected as there is so much snow in winter that keeping one's shoes on would create a mess. In other countries, such as Japan, the reasons may be religious and can be quite complex for the uninitiated. Being aware is important, but you can always ask and be guided by your host.

Travelling on public transport

While talking to others or speaking on the phone on buses and trains may be very common in many places around the world, it is not the case everywhere. In Switzerland, there are silent carriages in some trains where passengers don't speak to each other or on the phone. In Japan, people often avoid talking to each other on the phone when travelling by bus or train.

Over to you

Using the internet or films, find out about the conventions below in the country or countries where your target language is spoken.

How do different people address each other in different contexts?

....

....

....

....

What gifts do people usually take when visiting others?

....

....

....

....

How different are these conventions from your culture?

....

....

....

....

86 Non-verbal behaviour

In communicating with others, we do so not only with words, but also in other ways that don't draw on language itself, for example through body language. We're often not aware of our own body language, but if it's very different from the norm in the new context, we may be misunderstood or even cause offence. Here are some areas where there can be cultural differences in non-verbal behaviour.

In Tip 81 *Politeness*, we noted that changes in behaviour may result from severe public health dangers. It's important to be aware not only of local customs, but also directives from authorities that should be adhered to if there are health problems.

Proxemics

Proxemics refers to the space between people when speaking. In some cultures, it can be normal to stand very close to other people when speaking, whereas in others, people stand further apart. Either way, behaviour that is different can make people feel uncomfortable. If you're visiting another culture, read up on such issues and carefully observe what other people are doing.

Physical contact

Whether people touch each other when communicating varies from one culture to another. In some European cultures, colleagues shake hands every day, whereas in English-speaking cultures handshakes tend to be reserved for first meetings or special occasions. In some contexts, it may be inappropriate for a man to shake a woman's hand for religious reasons. In some Asian cultures, it's more common to bow than to shake hands.

Physical contact can also involve kissing and hugging, or not! In some cultures, men and women kiss other men and women on the cheeks, without there being any sexual connotation. However, this is usually when they know each other reasonably well or are family members. Hugging is also quite common in some cultures, yet not everyone wants to be hugged!

Eye contact

Cultures vary considerably in the way eye contact is viewed. Staring someone in the eye is likely to be inappropriate in most contexts, whereas looking directly in someone's eyes is polite when raising a glass together in many European cultures. However, in some Asian cultures, direct eye contact may be disrespectful.

Beware of gestures!

Many gestures that some cultures take for granted can be danger zones interculturally. The common thumbs-up sign, used in English-speaking and European contexts to mean someone has done well or the situation is positive, is offensive in some cultures.

Blowing your nose

In some Asian countries, it is considered extremely impolite to blow your nose in front of other people. The Chinese and Japanese, for example, find public nose blowing disgusting.

Differences between Yes and No

One important difference to be aware of is that while nodding your head means 'yes' in many cultures and shaking it means 'no', in Greece, Iran, Turkey, Bulgaria, Albania and Sicily a single nod of the head up (not down) indicates a 'no'.

Over to you

Watch a family series or drama online that is made in your target language and set in the culture you would like to visit or that interests you. Focus on cultural conventions in everyday social or professional life.

Do you notice any cultural conventions that are different from your own culture? Make some notes and, if possible, discuss your findings with someone from that culture.

....

....

....

....

....

....

....

....

87 Small talk / social talk

'Small talk', also called 'social talk', sometimes has connotations of superficiality, which is in fact a misconception. Small talk is commonly associated with brief greetings with neighbours and exchanges on topics such as the weather, but even such brief examples help to maintain good relations. In fact, small talk or social talk often involves lengthy discussions among family, friends and business partners on areas of common interest.

Such talk offers great opportunities to practise and improve your language skills, while also learning about the target culture. Some people are naturally more outgoing, and in some cultures it seems easier than in others to strike up a conversation with someone you don't know.

Here are some examples of places where you may be able to start talking to others if you're living or travelling in a country where your target language is spoken:

- waiting for public transport
- in a café or restaurant
- in the park while walking or exercising
- shopping
- walking around museums.

If you're learning the language in your own country you will have to be more imaginative in seeking opportunities for social talk. If you have a tandem partner you're probably already doing some social talk. Otherwise, there may be opportunities to meet people at local cultural groups, for example a 'Cercle français' (French Club) for French, which you could find online or through the local library or university.

What can you talk about if you're visiting a place where the target language is spoken? Well, if you naturally like to start a conversation with other people you probably won't have any problems, but otherwise you could:

- say you're visiting or new to the area and ask for advice about interesting places to visit
- admire someone's dog in the park and ask if a lot of people have dogs in the country or area
- say how much you like the area and ask for advice about amenities such as shops or anything else you need to know about

- comment on a painting or sculpture in a museum or art gallery. You could simply say how beautiful you find it and see where that leads.

If your language level is basic, you can imagine a scenario and practise it in advance. Remember to listen carefully to the person's response so you can follow up with a suitable response of your own. If one person doesn't respond, don't worry, you can try with someone else.

If you find people who have similar interests to you, or even share a passion, you will find social talk can really flow and will help you to make progress. In addition, as you talk, you can find out about the culture and observe what is similar to your home context and what is different. Keeping an open mind can be part of an exciting learning process in terms of both the language and the culture.

One word of warning though. Choose your topics carefully. Beware of topics that could cause conflict, such as politics or religion. Your aim is to practise using the language and learn about the culture. So choose neutral topics that tend to cross international borders well and are unlikely to offend people. For example, many people like talking about food. You can get people to recommend local dishes and in many countries the people are very proud of their cuisine. Similarly, music or the cinema can offer opportunities to compare what you like, and tend to be of interest worldwide. Hobbies, such as pets, dancing or travelling can also offer lots of opportunities for social talk. Beware though of subjects concerning money. In some cultures, asking someone how much they earn may be acceptable, but taboo in others. Indeed, you may find that some topics are considered appropriate for social talk in some cultures that would be avoided in your own.

In some cultures, asking personal questions is a way of getting to know people or keeping a conversation going, but in others this may be considered impolite. You may also need to be prepared to answer questions that you would not consider appropriate or learn ways to avoid answering them without offence. For example, if someone asks you a question such as 'How old are you?' or 'Why aren't you married?', and if you don't want to answer the question, you could smile and say 'Well, I'd rather not say!' It is, however, generally better not to ask such questions yourself until you know the person you are talking to and their culture well.

Over to you

If you're in a country where your target language is spoken, what opportunities are you going to use to practise the language and find out about the culture through social talk? Think of specific contexts and how to start a conversation. Make some notes.

....

....

....

....

....

....

....

If you're learning your target language in your own country, where might you be able to meet people to practise social talk?

....

....

....

....

....

....

....

88 Humour

Humour fulfils many functions and can be a helpful tool when speaking a foreign language and communicating with people from other cultures. Humour can, for example, help to put people at ease or overcome embarrassment, or even release tension in difficult situations.

When we speak of humour, we aren't thinking of jokes. Jokes are rather like scripted stories which are recounted by one person. There is often a 'punch line', at which point those listening should laugh. People who are good at telling jokes can be very amusing. However, in a foreign language and particularly in intercultural contexts, jokes can be a source of problems. For a start, jokes are often dependent on insider knowledge within a particular culture, so they may not be easy to understand outside that context. Some jokes may also be at the expense of other cultures or people, which clearly isn't the best option for intercultural understanding. In addition, many jokes depend on linguistic subtleties and may not translate easily, or the teller may unintentionally offend his or her audience through the use of inappropriate language.

However, a smile and a laugh may be enough to help you through a problem with understanding. Or a funny quip, perhaps at your own expense, can help to create a sense of solidarity or release tension. If you naturally use humour in your own language, you will probably find yourself automatically being humorous in your target language. If humour comes less easily to you, then you don't need to use it.

Remember too that humour can be a double-edged sword. Laughing at oneself is fine. Laughing at others or joking about them may well be offensive. Just as having a good laugh together can help people to bond, being sarcastic or teasing others can damage relationships.

Over to you

Have you found yourself using humour in your target language? How did this feel and how did people react?

....

....

....

Have you ever had the experience of noticing that humour can be different in another culture?

....

....

....

When communicating with people from another culture in your target language, try to identify speakers who use humour effectively. Observe what they are doing and how it helps the conversation.

Make notes on anything you notice.

....

....

....

....

....

89 Cultural guides

One of the best ways to learn about the culture of your target language is to find an 'insider'. This could be someone who was brought up in a country where the language is spoken or who has spent a lot of time there. It could be someone in your home country who has either immigrated or who travels regularly to your country.

Tandem partners are obvious choices – see Tip 16 *Learn with a tandem partner*. Working with a tandem partner, either face to face or online, will give you the opportunity to exchange information on a regular basis with someone who knows the culture that interests you. At home, you can find people from all around the world on university campuses, both staff and students. Offering student accommodation or getting involved in cultural activities or trips could be a good way to meet people from other countries. Such contacts can be ideal cultural guides and may also appreciate having you as a cultural guide if they have only recently arrived in your country.

People who are bilingual and bicultural may be particularly helpful as they often have an understanding of subtle cultural differences in more than one culture and can easily inform you of typical pitfalls in intercultural communication from the perspective of both of their cultural backgrounds. Such people may come from international families, with parents of different nationalities.

Over to you

Where could you find a cultural guide?

....

....

Here are some examples of useful information you could ask your cultural guide about. You might like to make some notes on their answers.

How should you address older people? Should you use their first names?

....

....

What could you take if you're invited to someone's home?

....

....

Are there any interests or hobbies shared by many people in the country or countries where your target language is spoken?

....

....

Can you think of other information you would like to ask your cultural guide about?

....

....

....

....

....

90 Lingua franca communication

A lingua franca is a common language used between speakers who don't share the same mother tongue or culture.

There are many lingua francas, for example, Arabic, Mandarin Chinese, English, French, Spanish and Swahili. These are languages that are used in a number of different countries, other than simply in the areas in which they originated. They are sometimes called pluricentric languages as they may be used in many different geographical contexts, but their speakers don't share the same cultures. French, for example, is spoken in many African countries and used by these countries for commerce with other nations such as China.

In early European universities, Latin was the language of communication and instruction even though it wasn't the native language of any of the students. Today, English is used in many contexts as the lingua franca of business and for international research. But it's certainly not the only contemporary lingua franca.

As speakers of a lingua franca don't share the same cultural norms, they may have fewer expectations concerning socio-cultural behaviour. Research shows they adapt or accommodate to each other in terms of what is appropriate in particular contexts. They tend to be flexible and accept that in any group of lingua franca speakers there may be people from very different cultures and with different language levels. With the focus on the message rather than the language itself, they are also good at overcoming communication problems and achieving mutual understanding.

If you're involved in international business, international research or just sitting on a beach somewhere in Europe, you may well find yourself among people of a range of nationalities speaking a lingua franca. If this is the case, you will find that the emphasis is on getting your message across and being comprehensible, rather than worrying if your grammar is correct. Of course, in any context, you will need a threshold level to be able to speak to others, but you may find there is less pressure in terms of correctness or cultural norms than with native speakers.

In cultural terms, you may also find middle ground with participants, perhaps adapting to the local context and drawing on their own and others' cultural conventions. So there will be less emphasis on learning the norms of a specific culture as you would have to if you were integrating into one culture. You may also find the speakers take time to speak to each other about their different cultures, which can, of course, be very enriching.

Over to you

Is your target language considered to be a lingua franca? You can do some online research to find out.

....

....

Are you likely to use your target language as a lingua franca? ....

Here are two examples from personal experience:

- negotiating a hire car in German when on holiday in Greece
- social talk in German while having a massage in Hungary

When might you use your target language as a lingua franca, i.e. with people who aren't native speakers of that language?

....

....

....

....

....

Or do you already use your target language as a lingua franca? ....

If so, what can you learn from this type of communication?

....

....

....

....

....

Key points

In this section, we have considered a number of aspects of communicating in different cultures. Here are some key points to remember:

- It's important to bear in mind that what is appropriate may differ considerably from one context to another.
- Awareness of cultural differences in politeness or appropriate behaviour is important to ensure smooth intercultural communication.
- Some languages have polite forms built into their grammar and having some knowledge of this is important, even if they take time to master.
- There are both individual and cultural differences in communication styles, for example in relation to directness or indirectness, so it's helpful to be aware of one's own individual communication style and how this may differ from what is common in the target culture.
- Social rituals, for example when visiting someone's house, can vary from one culture to another; doing some research on what is expected in different contexts can be very helpful.
- Cultural differences in non-verbal communication such as gestures or physical contact can easily lead to misunderstandings or offence.
- Social talk can help you to find areas of common ground and compare cultural differences.
- If humour comes naturally to you, it can help to put people at ease, but it can be a double-edged sword and should be used with care.
- If in doubt, ask, and if possible find a cultural guide or insider.

My own take-home notes on Communicating in different cultures

....

....

....

....

....

....

J Tips from successful language learners

We do not learn from experience … we learn from reflecting on experience.

John Dewey (1859–1952)

What better way of learning than reflecting on what successful language learners have done in studying a range of languages, often for very different reasons, with different approaches and in varied contexts?

In this section, you will find 17 case studies of language learners whose ages range from their 20s to their 80s. Many of them were exposed to other languages as children, which in some cases led to an interest in languages. All of them began learning a language at school, although not all of them found what they learnt at school particularly interesting or helpful. What unites them all, however, is that in the long term they have grown to enjoy learning and using foreign languages and, above all, have been successful in language learning.

You will see that while most of them have reached a high level in at least one foreign language, this isn't the case with all the languages they have learnt. In fact, it may be an assumption amongst people with little experience or success in language learning that you have to aim for perfection, whereas this is definitely not the case. We hope to have shown in this book that being able to meet your specific needs should be your main goal. But you will probably find that learning to communicate in another language is not only valuable in terms of meeting basic needs, but can also open doors to new cultures and enriching intercultural experiences. So you may well find you get hooked on language learning and decide to go on to higher levels or indeed to another language.

Some of the case studies here include learners who became fascinated by languages at school and made languages the base of their careers, for example in teaching or translating. For others, learning languages later in life became a means to an end and an essential element in their work. We should emphasise once again that, although most of the people who feature in these case studies have been to university this is clearly not a prerequisite for language learning. All over the world many people with different and varied educational backgrounds have mastered a second – or indeed third or fourth – language so well that they can operate in it both at work and in their social lives.

The tips in this section are not quite like those in other sections. Each of the people in the case studies we present offers his or her own advice directly to you but you may also find that reading about their experiences suggests ideas that you would find useful in your own context.

We hope you will find their 'stories' interesting and inspiring!

Aims of this section

In this section, we encourage you to explore and reflect on a range of language learners' profiles and consider what has made them successful.

The case studies in this section show you:

- many different reasons why people learn foreign languages
- how different people approach language learning
- ways of organising the time spent on language learning
- enjoyable and useful activities for language learning
- the benefits of technology
- the importance of exposure and practice
- that mistakes are not bad
- that learning languages opens doors: intercultural, professional and romantic!

In this section, there are no 'Over to you' tasks or questions at the end of each case study. We suggest you note or highlight points of interest in each case study and then list them in the Key points at the end of the section.

91 Rae's story

I'm 22 and I'm Chinese. I lived all my life in China before moving to Spain to pursue a Master's degree in marketing a year ago.

The languages in my life

I speak Chinese, English and Spanish. Chinese is my mother tongue and my most frequently used language in my personal life. However, I've been having all my classes and talking to many of my friends in English ever since I moved to Spain, while using Spanish in shops and for other routine interactions with locals.

I started to learn English at primary school at the age of seven. However, the teaching method at school was mainly focused on reading and writing, with a lack of practice in listening and speaking. So I took some online English courses to practise English conversation in high school and that was when I made some real progress. In the meantime, I watched plenty of British TV series from the BBC and so forth with bilingual subtitles, which primarily contributed to my growing interest in English and building up vocabulary. While I was doing my first degree, I tried to make foreign friends whenever I could and joined a couple of international programmes where transnational interaction was required, enjoying the exchange of languages and cultures. I also started to watch English videos without subtitles when I was preparing for IELTS exams, which I'd say brought my English to another level.

Spanish came into my life when I signed up for a language course a couple of years ago in a private institute. I've taken classes on and off since then, but didn't really put in much effort until I started to teach myself by watching Spanish videos and making an effort to find Spanish speakers to talk to.

What I enjoy about learning languages

What I enjoy most about learning languages is that I'm able to embrace different cultures from an internal perspective. I can read and watch original content and talk to native speakers. This is also what I find most useful in learning languages as it involves immersing yourself entirely in other languages, although this has to come after you've mastered the basics of the language in question.

An ongoing project

I'm still working on my Spanish, which is around intermediate level at the moment. I speak to tandem partners and watch Spanish videos every day.

Tips for language learners

I know it sounds a bit of a cliché, but well, 'Practice makes perfect' is the only truth about learning a language. Practise with people who have already mastered the language and read/watch content in that language even if it's torturous at the beginning.

A humorous anecdote

I remember one time when I was asking a Spanish speaker if he liked onion, which in Spanish is 'cebolla'. Unfortunately, I said 'cabeza' instead, which means 'head' in Spanish. He paused for a few seconds after he heard what I said and was probably wondering why I would want to know if he liked human heads. That made us both laugh.

92 Cao Cao's story

I'm 23 and Chinese. I'm studying in the US, majoring in Finance, and I will get my Master's degree this year. I've spent most of my life in China, but before coming to the US to study, I took part in a summer exchange programme which gave me the chance to study in Switzerland. I also had an earlier internship in the US.

The languages in my life

I speak Chinese and English, and a little Russian. Chinese is my mother tongue, so I learnt it from childhood. I use it every day to communicate with my family and friends; I learnt English at school and university and studied it mainly with textbooks and preparing for exams. I use English mostly to communicate with teachers, colleagues and other students. I speak Russian because I'm interested in the language. I learnt it when studying for my Bachelor's degree in Shanghai, through online classes.

What I enjoy about learning languages

I really enjoy learning languages and find languages helpful mainly for two reasons. Firstly, I think languages help me communicate better with people from different countries, so I can realise how their life is different from Chinese people's lives. Secondly, through learning languages, I can understand specific cultures better. I admit I'm curious by nature and I'm very eager to understand other cultures, especially concerning history.

An ongoing project

I'm still working on learning English now. I watch CNN news every day to review information related to current affairs within the US.

Tips for foreign language learners

I think when you're learning a foreign language, the most important thing is memorising vocabulary. Only if you know as many words as you can learn, can you make communication simple with people who speak that language. That is the initial step when studying a foreign language and new experiences will enhance your enthusiasm to study that language more.

A humorous anecdote

A couple of years ago, when I was an intern at an American firm, I and my American colleagues went to a Chinese restaurant. As we waited for food, they asked what my father did. I answered: 'My father sells drugs for a living.' Suddenly, everyone fell silent. Later, I learnt that 'selling drugs' has more meanings than I thought as it also means 'selling narcotics', when what I wanted to say was 'sells medicine'.

93 Henrik's story

I'm 26 and I'm Swedish. I was brought up in Stockholm and have moved several times for work and for studies between places in Sweden and France. For the last three years I have been in Paris and I will be there until summer, when I'm finishing my degree in architecture.

The languages in my life

I started learning English early and continued all through to high school. Since then, it has always been an important language for me and I've improved my English skills over time by constant exposure and using it often to take in information and communicate.

I had French lessons in my last years of school, but I only reached an elementary level. However, after an exchange year in Lyon, my French improved rapidly as I got to know many people through using the language.

Since living in Paris, I've been both working and studying, alternating a lot between English and French. French is my everyday language for going about the city, speaking to teachers and when meeting new people. But my weak writing skills have meant it has been a constant struggle since I started my Master's in architecture. Progressing 'on the job', I've asked many friends for help and I'm constantly looking up vocabulary and grammar rules when writing a text. I've developed a somewhat more solid base, but my version of the language is still something my French friends can laugh about. For some reason, when I'm speaking without thinking, all objects take the feminine form 'la'... a Freudian slip or just pure laziness?

English follows me in my everyday life too, keeping in touch with friends and hanging out with the many international people in Paris.

What I enjoy about learning languages

Even though it has taken a long time to be able to 'be myself' in English, and at the moment in French, I have found it very enriching to meet people and take part in their culture through their language. I can also sense that I'm behaving differently with the different languages, and I like the idea that there are several versions of myself, responding to different situations.

An ongoing project

I have several writing assignments at my school of architecture and my current focus is on the choice of words and the use of language, which is very important for conveying the right message. In my current project I'm faced with the exercise of jumping between languages; the information about the building site is in Swedish, the written research paper is in English and the oral presentations and discussions are in French. The juggling of the languages is very interesting, and it has made me cautious about not only 'false friends', but also how a slightly different meaning or emphasis in a word can make an expression richer in one language, or do the opposite, even giving the expression another meaning.

Tips for language learners

I've found it important to always be curious and take a few extra moments to look into the small things you stumble upon and do not quite understand. It's easy to fall into habits, not questioning how you or others use a language, but taking a step back for a few seconds has allowed me to find small language lessons, both with friends and in a work environment.

A humorous anecdote

In some languages, such as French, it's hard to know how a word is spelt after just hearing it. There is a common expression you use in French when you're very tired, 'Je suis crevé', literally, 'I am flat.' Using it in oral situations was never a problem, but when once writing it in a group text message, I accidentally got a new nickname, not helped that I have red hair. I wrote 'Je suis crevette', literally, 'I am a shrimp.'

94 Clarissa's story

I'm 29 and British. I grew up in the UK and studied languages for my undergraduate degree. After working in translation and language teaching in the UK, I moved to France. For the last couple of years, I've been living in France, working and continuing my further education in languages, completing a Master's in translation and recently starting a PhD in linguistics and translation.

The languages in my life

I speak three languages well and can hold a conversation in one other. English is my mother tongue, and I use it with friends and family, as well as for reading and research. I studied French and Spanish to degree level and I currently use French on a daily basis (both at home and at work) and occasionally Spanish. I can understand and speak a small amount of Italian, as my partner is Italian. I use my limited Italian when we visit friends and family in Italy.

I learnt French at school from the age of 10 and then continued learning French at university in both the UK and France. I'm still learning now, but I would say exposure from living in France as well as studying in France has definitely helped improve my French.

Spanish was covered briefly at school, but I didn't 'properly' learn it until I started my undergraduate degree. I spent one year in Spain teaching English as part of my degree and improved my Spanish language skills dramatically.

Since meeting my partner, I've been passively learning Italian through trips to Italy and listening to conversations, as well as reading books.

What I enjoy about learning languages

I've always enjoyed speaking French and being in France. When I was little, we used to go to France for our family holidays, so I imagine this helped kindle my love of languages too. I particularly like being able to use knowledge of one language to help understand another. What's most helpful about learning languages is being able to understand and communicate with others, which can create opportunities not only for work but also for new friendships.

An ongoing project

I'm working on improving my Italian to be able to communicate with my partner's friends and family. I've read some short books in Italian (most recently Roald Dahl), and often my partner and I spend one day a week speaking Italian at home.

Tips for language learners

I would say the best way to learn a language is to try and spend some time in a country or a context where you can practise the language in your daily life. I think full immersion in another country is truly the best way but if this isn't possible, try to find a context where you can have full immersion for a limited time, for example attending a language class and using the language with fellow students outside class. Find an activity that you enjoy doing in your native language and see if you can continue to do this activity with others in a foreign language or foreign country. As you already know how to do the activity, you can focus on learning new vocabulary and chatting to others.

A humorous anecdote

On one of my first trips to Italy with some English friends, we went for a coffee. I wanted a milky coffee (or 'latte' as we like to call them in the UK), so asked for a *latte*. The waitress looked a bit confused but took the order anyway. It turned out that latte was just a glass of hot milk. I quickly learnt that something I might think is Italian doesn't necessarily mean it's known in Italy! When I'm in Italy, I now always ask for a 'caffè latte', or when in doubt, a 'cappuccino'!

95 John's story

I'm 32 years old and British. I was born in Switzerland to British parents and we moved to the UK when I was two. I grew up in south-west England, studied philosophy at undergraduate level, and then worked in London while doing a Master's in politics. After that I completed a PhD in international relations, then did a post-doc for a year in the US, and am now a university professor in the fields of security and global affairs in the Netherlands. I recently married my partner of seven years.

The languages in my life

I speak English, Arabic and Dutch. English is my mother tongue and I use it professionally. I also use Arabic professionally as my research focuses on the Arab world (mainly the Gulf states and Egypt). I'm learning Dutch at the moment. I learnt French and German to school-leaving certificate level but have largely forgotten them.

My approach to language learning

I took some beginner courses in Arabic while working in London. I began studying seriously at the start of my PhD, with two intensive courses in Oman (one to two months) and extensive self-study (three hours a day). Later, I had online and in-person weekly tandem partners and paid online lessons. This study was funded by my PhD programme.

For Dutch, I began learning Dutch when I moved to the Netherlands. I've had weekly small-group classes organised by my university. My level of spoken Dutch isn't high but I have good reading comprehension.

For Arabic, after learning the script and grammar (through websites and a textbook, as well as the lessons mentioned above), I improved my comprehension most by listening to the radio and reading – first short newspaper articles and then short stories and novels. I also watch films and TV series to learn different dialects, although these are almost like entirely separate languages to learn.

I've also used a website to learn the rules of Dutch grammar explained in English, even before I had any significant vocabulary. Unlike Arabic, my exposure to Dutch is largely through conversations in my workplace and TV shows, which I watch with subtitles in Dutch – I find this helpful.

For both Arabic and Dutch I've used apps to learn vocabulary – for Arabic, the 5,000 most common Arabic words on *Anki*, and for Dutch, 3,000 common Dutch words on *Dutchwords*.

What I enjoy about learning languages

I enjoy speaking to people and understanding the languages of countries I visit. I feel it's important as a native English speaker to make an effort, even if it's rarely rewarded given the extent of the English language across the world. I enjoy reading fiction, linguistics and grammar, and learning how the rules of languages work. I also enjoy etymology and tracing the meaning of words across languages.

An ongoing project

I have a tandem partner to improve my Egyptian Arabic dialect, and make an effort to read and listen regularly.

I have lessons in Dutch at work.

Tips for language learners

There are no short cuts – it takes time and effort. Learn words by rote because you can get the grammar significantly wrong and still communicate. But also learn the grammar! Find things you enjoy watching, reading or doing in that language to help motivate you.

A humorous anecdote

On my first intensive Arabic course in Oman I went to one of the few hotel bars in Muscat with some friends. Eager to try my Arabic, I said 'as-salam alaikum' to the Omanis at the table next to me. I didn't then know that this is a particularly religious greeting in Oman (unlike in Egypt, for example, where it's used formally in non-religious contexts), and the fact that they were at a hotel bar meant that it was extremely incongruous – which probably explained their odd looks and laughter in response.

96 Aleksandrina's story

I'm 39, originally Bulgarian, and have lived in five different countries. I was born and raised in Sofia but due to political and economic turbulence my family migrated to Nigeria when I was 11. I then studied Political Science in Sofia University, followed by an MA at the Central European University in Budapest, Hungary. After returning to Bulgaria and working there for seven years, I moved to New York where I studied documentary film and created my own film production company which creates everything from animation to documentaries. For the past three years, I've been living in France where I continue to work as a film director/producer.

The languages in my life

I speak and understand six languages to various degrees. Bulgarian is my mother tongue, I speak English fluently, French intermediately, I understand most Russian and can speak some and finally, I've learnt but don't know Spanish and German well. I started learning English in pre-school. When you come from a small country like Bulgaria (Bulgarian is only spoken by some seven million people), everyone learns a lot of languages early on. I then went to an American high school for three years in Nigeria, studied my MA and post-graduate degree in English, worked and lived in NYC for seven years. Around 90% of my work is currently in English. I learnt Russian – against my will as it was mandatory when I was in primary school. Then in high school we were also left with no choice but to learn Russian as there were too many Russian teachers. I hated the experience but am grateful that I understand it. I took Spanish and German on my own when I was wondering where to go for my university. I did three levels of German at the Goethe Institute, the last one during a summer camp in Berlin, which was a lot of fun. And finally French, the language I thought I'd never have to learn, is something I'm currently undertaking as destiny has a good sense of humour and France is where I've ended up.

What I enjoy about learning languages

I love communicating with different people and cultures, and learning local languages is the most authentic and respectful way to do that. English is the international language of business nowadays, so most people speak it. But learning smaller languages is rewarding as they bring you closer to others' culture and challenge your brain to rewire its usual way of processing information.

An ongoing project

I'm currently learning French, which has been the most difficult language for me. You would think that I'd be fluent in over three years but there is something about the complexity of French grammar and spelling that makes the process especially difficult for me. I listen to a lot of French, including TV series and films, so I'm getting better at understanding it, but I can't find my words when speaking. Part of the problem is that I work in English and communicate in Bulgarian at home, so I practise French very little and my level is stuck at small talk around dog walks by the canal next to my flat.

Tips for language learners

Start speaking the new language right away and don't worry about grammar or pronunciation at first! The more fun it is for you, the faster you will learn.

97 Kasia's story

I'm in my early 40s and Polish. As an adolescent, I moved to Kinshasa for four years for my dad's work. I've also lived in Canada, where I did my Master's degree and met my German husband. We subsequently lived in Berlin and then in France and Switzerland. I did my doctoral thesis at the Warsaw School of Economics and post-doc studies in Geneva. Since then, I've worked in Switzerland. I'm a full professor in cross-cultural management.

The languages in my life

I speak Polish, French, English and German. I use Polish with my kids, my Polish family and our nanny. I don't have Polish friends in Switzerland or France but I have a Polish network. About 80% of my work is in English, both oral and written. I also speak English as a lingua franca with my husband. I use French, chiefly oral, at work for about 20% of the time.

My mom was an English teacher and I went to the American School of Kinshasa. When we went back to Poland, I took several international exams, including Cambridge Proficiency.

When I lived in Kinshasa, all my informal interactions with peers were in English but occasionally in French with friends and the local community. I continued learning French at university for four years, taking advanced French for four hours a week. I studied at HEC Montreal, with the majority of courses in French. All my informal interactions were in French.

I started to learn German when I met my husband (in Montreal we spoke French), then one year later, I took an intensive course at a private school for a month and reached B2. The kids' education is in German. I listen to them speaking to my husband. I also help them with school work, so I need to read a lot in German, but I write very little. I read the Swiss German press and watch Swiss German news and I use Deepl online translation software.

My approach to language learning

Although I enjoy speaking all these languages, my motivation for the effort involved in learning is instrumental. For German, my aim is firstly inclusiveness. For example, to avoid being excluded in family conversations. Secondly, I need German for the kids, so I can help them at school and German is so important for them.

French has been important for me to be autonomous as my job is in Switzerland. French is also essential in terms of career development, such as in being more efficient in developing local networks. Finally, English is natural for me: as a Pole, you must be fluent in English.

What I enjoy about learning languages

I enjoy using foreign languages so much, even if my mastery isn't 100% or even 80%, but I love interacting with people, and the more languages I speak, the more people I can interact with.

An ongoing project

I continue working on both French and German. For French, my aim is to reduce the number of mistakes I make when writing, if possible to zero. For German, I'm working mainly on continuing to extend my vocabulary and also learn more Swiss German nuances.

Tips for language learners

Have a vision – why you need a language, how a new language can improve your professional or social interactions.

Be smart – the moment you're surrounded by a language you don't know, you need to learn it. My work involves working in academic and corporate settings in China. I don't think I'm 'smart' as I haven't learnt Chinese … well, I learnt for a semester and had some private classes in China. The moment the kids don't rely so much on me because of their age, I might start learning Chinese again.

98 Rike's story

I'm 42 years old and Portuguese. I lived with my grandparents in Portugal until I was 11. After primary school I moved to Bern in Switzerland to join my parents, who were working there. I went to secondary school in Bern and then did a two-year course in electrotechnics. After that, I worked in an Italian restaurant before returning to Portugal where I got married and worked in the building industry. I also worked in Spain in the same field. Shortly after my first daughter was born, I returned to Switzerland, also to work in the building industry.

The languages in my life

I speak five languages. Portuguese is my mother tongue. Lessons at my school in Bern were in German and I did French at school. I also learnt it studying on my own and speaking with friends. I learnt Italian when I was taking the course in electrotechnics and also by speaking with friends. When I worked in Spain I also learnt the language there. I use both French and German every day and sometimes the other languages at work, speaking to my bosses, the staff and clients. I'm a foreman for a big Swiss building company in a bilingual city. I speak Italian with some friends and Spanish when I go on holiday to Spanish-speaking countries. At home, I speak Portuguese and also when I return to Portugal.

It's easy for me to get on with people, particularly clients at work, as I can switch to their language. This is particularly so as there are three main official languages in Switzerland: French, German and Italian and I'm fortunate enough to speak all three. French is the dominant language in the city where I work, although it's bilingual. But if I'm working for a client who doesn't speak French I enjoy switching to German or Italian.

What I enjoy about learning languages

I really enjoyed learning the languages I speak. I liked learning the verbs in each of the languages I studied. I also found the way German is spoken interesting as the word order often seems to be 'the opposite' of the other languages.

An ongoing project

I'm not learning another language at the moment, but I'd like to learn to speak English as it's a universal language.

Tips for language learners

Build up a rich and varied vocabulary, learn how to conjugate the verbs and, most importantly, learn how to form a sentence.

99 Steve's story

I'm 44 and British. I was formerly a teacher of English as a Foreign Language (EFL) in Portugal and Japan. Now I work in language assessment in the UK. I led a quiet life until I was offered a job as an accountant. I suddenly realised this wasn't for me and decided that what I really wanted was to experience life abroad instead.

The languages in my life

I studied French at secondary school. I began enthusiastically enough, but I think I was too self-conscious to succeed at that age. I regret it now, but I do speak three languages, at least to some extent. I'm a native speaker of English; I use Japanese to converse with my wife's family and others on biennial trips to Japan. The third language is Portuguese, but I don't get much chance to practise it save for very occasional interactions, mostly online.

My approach to language learning

Living in a culture where the target language is spoken, as an English teacher in Portugal, I taught myself Portuguese, in part by reading the daily football newspaper. I found my pre-existing contextual knowledge very effective scaffolding when reading, say, English Premier League match reports. When I lived in Japan for four years, I learnt Japanese from students and teachers in school, then from my wife's family, as this was necessary to function effectively in society. Many other cultural contexts were helpful in acquiring the language, such as karaoke, public baths and sumo.

What I enjoy about learning languages

I enjoy forming and sustaining connections with people, which would otherwise not be possible.

Tips for language learners

I think it's all about finding a source of motivation and using the language for something you're interested in, as I did in Portugal and Japan. I didn't succeed in the somewhat theoretical language lessons back in secondary school, where exam results were (to my teenage self) the only incentive to learn.

A humorous anecdote

Whilst trying to do the right thing, my 2001-vintage Japanese grammar was not quite up to the job and so I ended up *telling* rather than asking my father-in-law-to-be that I was going to marry his daughter. I think I may have got away with it, however!

100 Ken's story

I'm 47 and British. I currently work for an examinations board in the UK. I used to be a teacher of English as a Foreign Language (EFL) and taught in Italy, Japan, Slovakia and the UK.

The languages in my life

I speak Italian and Korean. I also speak a little Japanese and learnt French and German at school. I had to study French from 9 to 14. I was actually very good, but foolishly switched to German because I preferred German football. Languages weren't a priority in my school so I didn't get to grips with German as much and ended up less fluent in a second language than I would have been if I'd stuck with French for a few more years.

I studied Italian and Japanese while working in those countries and I'm studying Korean at home with my partner and her family and friends. For Italian, it's only for holidays now and my language level has dropped considerably. I study Korean because my partner is from Seoul and our young son is bilingual. I'm trying to use Korean for everyday activities.

My partner reads Korean books to our son at bedtime and I listen in and ask him to explain what I don't understand. I find it much easier to remember what he says in Korean.

What I enjoy about learning languages

I enjoy the feeling of being able to communicate with people in their first language, but I do find it a struggle. I find it helpful to do remedial repetition until I'm confident with the syntax and pronunciation. I read cartoons and children's books with my son – you get the visual input plus a light reading load.

Tips for language learners

Be very patient and set small achievable goals. Try to do flexible sessions of as little as ten minutes a day every day, rather than setting aside longer sessions. This is because you only feel guilty and discouraged if something comes up which prevents you from doing a long study session and it's easier to make a ten-minute habit stick.

A humorous anecdote

I got into trouble once because I pronounced the Korean honorific 님 (nim – used to honour people with respected positions, e.g. teachers, managers) as 놈 (nom – used to question someone's parentage).

101 Jean-Paul's story

I'm Swiss, from the French-speaking part, and I'll soon be stepping into my sixth decade. I've spent most of my career in research and development in the food industry. At one point, my company offered me a position in the UK, where I subsequently spent nearly nine years with my family. During this time, I also had the opportunity to do a Master's degree in food science. I'm used to working within an international environment where English is the common language.

The languages in my life

I speak two languages. French is my mother tongue and I use English mainly at work. I enjoy using English with English-speaking friends and when travelling abroad. I also have some basics in German from school. As a Swiss native, we have to learn another national language, but I never had a chance to improve it.

I started learning German at school when I was 12 and English during my training. I also had English tuition funded by my employer. Unfortunately, I felt incapable of learning more than a few basics as I always struggled at being intellectually focused. If I was a kid nowadays, I would probably be diagnosed with some attention deficit disorder. In fact, I learnt by immersion and I was amazed to find myself fluent in English after two or three years living in the UK.

Because I have travel plans, I recently started learning Spanish at evening classes but gave up because learning through immersion suits me much better.

What I enjoy about learning languages

Living in England was a wonderful oportunity to discover another culture. Mastering English gives you an open door to the world as it's the main international language. You can travel almost everywhere and find someone to communicate with in English.

Tips for language learners

Go and live for a while in a country where the language you want to learn is spoken. Most importantly, try to integrate into the social life.

A humorous anecdote

I had just arrived in the UK and my English tutor advised me when attending business meetings to sit with someone who could help me. Once in a meeting an Irishman said something and I said to my English colleague: 'Alex, please, I don't understand what he said.' He answered: 'Don't worry, me neither ...'. Then I learnt to enjoy the variety of English accents.

102 Nadya's story

I'm in my early sixties and I grew up in Russia, that vast country that stretches from Europe to Asia.

The languages in my life

To start school was exciting, as it is for any child, I suppose. I had a good first teacher and was impatient to start learning a foreign language. In grade six at last we got to choose English or French and French was the obvious choice for me. It turned out that it was a small language for our big country, with some disadvantages like a shortage of teachers. One year (my eighth grade) the school couldn't provide a French teacher for us and in the end it was decided that the pupils who had been doing French should start learning English instead. I must say it was a very confusing year for my foreign language learning. In the following two years at school I was able to continue with French again.

Aged 20 and a bit, I left my homeland with my studies completed and an engineering degree in my pocket. Then followed some years in an Arabic-speaking country as well as about three years in England, studying English and getting a Master's in engineering. Now I live in Sweden and recently it dawned on me that I've been living here longer than I lived in my original homeland.

My mother tongue is Russian. I speak it with my relatives and my son, but not often enough I feel. I speak Swedish and English well enough (I believe), however there's always room for improvement, as you realise there's always more to learn. I learnt both English and Swedish at language schools with good teachers.

I can speak and understand a little Arabic, but unfortunately I haven't used it for quite some time now and I'm sorry to say it's a sad example of how important it is to practise the language if you want to keep it alive. There was no school I could go to to learn Arabic, so the method I used was to listen and try to understand and then repeat to the best of my ability.

What I enjoy about learning languages

I enjoy the challenge of learning a new language even though it's hard at the beginning and it takes some time before one can speak it reasonably well. Usually the journey there is worth it anyway. The satisfaction and joy when you say a sentence correctly and then the small steps that lead one to more complex understanding of language – you can talk to people in their own language and make some new friends along the way.

Tips for language learners

I would suggest (if one has the possibility) spending time in a country where the language is spoken and attending a school with the purpose of learning the language. To use all the opportunities to practise: listening, reading, speaking … almost forget your first language or, for some time at least, reduce your use of it to a minimum. Not to despair when sometimes you feel you're not making progress, because you will be, even if it doesn't always feel that way.

A humorous anecdote

In Swedish there are long and short vowels and the meaning of a word changes completely depending on the pronunciation. This can lead to embarrassing situations, which I've experienced a few times. For example, you might receive a glass of water when you ask for an ice cream. There are worse examples than this one, which are probably not suitable here.

103 Hazel's story

I'm 68 and I'm British. My father was British and my mother Chinese. They settled in the UK in 1948 in the south of England, where I went to school.

The languages in my life

My parents always used English in the home. They feared not having English as a first language might be a disadvantage for me, so (sadly) I wasn't brought up bilingually. Nevertheless, as a child I did acquire 'kitchen and bathroom' Chinese at home.

But I now speak three languages. English is my first language, which I use for most purposes. I speak Mandarin Chinese when in China, with Chinese family and in some China-related work contexts. I also speak Italian with limited fluency and use it occasionally when in Italy for travel or work purposes. I studied Italian as a gap-year student living and working in Rome and then later as an adult, taking evening classes in the UK.

I didn't show any particular aptitude for languages as a child, but studied French to school-leaving certificate level, albeit without gaining the ability to really communicate.

I resisted the idea of studying Mandarin and Chinese culture generally 'just because of heritage'. So I studied English literature and philosophy as an undergraduate and for a Master's degree, then went to Harvard on a scholarship as a 'special student', where there was a flexible system in place to pursue varied academic interests. I had taken Mandarin at evening classes when I was 18 so at Harvard I took advantage of the opportunity to study Mandarin systematically for the first time, both for writing and speaking.

This was a belated beginning of a demanding, slow, frustrating but rewarding challenge. Two years later, after the end of the Cultural Revolution and then the death of Mao, I was able to go to China as a British Council scholar. I spent six weeks at the Languages Institute in Beijing and then a year in Manchuria as a graduate student at Liaoning University. I taught English language and literature at the Languages Institute in Beijing for a couple of years. On return to the UK, I moved to Cambridge initially as sinological librarian at the University Library. My career has involved a combination of China-related educational work and teaching, training and assessment in the world of teaching English as a Foreign Language (EFL).

What I enjoy about learning languages

I enjoy seeing the world in a different way; challenging the brain, and in my mixed heritage context, exploring different aspects of identity. I also enjoy reading novels in the target language. In practice, I've found the need to communicate in the target language provides a pressing reason to put in a great deal of hard work in learning it!

Tips for language learners

Immerse yourself as fully as possible in the linguistic environment and if that isn't possible, read avidly and watch films.

A humorous anecdote

As a child, because of the 'kitchen and bathroom' first language, I was unable to tell teachers in English that I needed to go to the bathroom and had much discomfort accordingly, exacerbated by extreme shyness which led teachers to assume I had no English. That's not what my parents had had in mind in not making me bilingual!

104 Victoria's story

I'm 73 and British. I live in France, but grew up in the UK, moved to Israel in the mid-1960s, where I spent about five years, followed by Algeria for a year and a half, before coming to France in 1976. I taught English as a Foreign Language (EFL) until I retired.

The languages in my life

I speak two languages well, my mother tongue which is English, and French. I speak three others – Hebrew, Spanish and German – to varying degrees, but I wouldn't say well!

French has become my main language. I use it every day for nearly everything, communicating with friends and neighbours, shopping and life's admin (taxes, dentists, house-painters, paying bills, etc.), radio and internet (online newspapers) and cultural activities (reading novels, theatre, cinema). I use English mostly on the phone to English-speaking friends and for reading UK newspapers online when UK news is important. I very rarely use Hebrew and Spanish now. As for German, I read an online newspaper every day.

I studied French for several years at secondary school in the UK, where, back in the 1950s and 60s, teaching methods centred on word lists, conjugation tables and translation. Then I learnt informally from living in Algeria, where French was still widely spoken in the 1970s, and France.

I went to Hebrew evening classes once a week in the UK for about a year before moving to Israel, and once there I spent several months at an Ulpan, an intensive Hebrew language programme intended for new immigrants to the country, and then reinforced what I'd learnt in daily life.

I taught myself Spanish to 'tourist survival level' in the 1980s, via coursebooks and recordings which I listened to on a Walkman (remember those!), and reading a weekly magazine. I practised it on visits to Spanish-speaking countries.

I started learning German five years ago. I go to an hour and a half class every week, and to a self-help group for an hour and a half every week. I also read a German-language newspaper online for 10 to 15 minutes every day, and at least once a week do an episode of an online German video course on the Deutsche Welle (German international broadcaster) website.

What I enjoy about learning languages

French wasn't my favourite subject at school, and it was only years later that I appreciated how formal learning of the basics was a great help when I started using it. Hebrew and Spanish were more enjoyable, perhaps because I chose to learn them – I liked the sounds and intonation and learning to produce these myself. In the case of Hebrew, I also loved learning the alphabet and the script – you read and write from right to left – there was something almost artistic about making the shapes, and it was satisfying to be able to write even a postcard to Hebrew-speaking friends, and read what they sent me. Visiting Spanish-speaking countries and understanding and being able to communicate even a little were small triumphs every time. Even minor successes encourage you to keep going. Now, with learning German, I enjoy its correspondences with English, for example the word for 'glove' is 'Handschuh', unforgettable! Recognising words and expressions in German films is encouraging too, and I'm enjoying discovering German cinema.

An ongoing project

I'm learning German, really out of curiosity as English is part of the Germanic language family, and I wanted to see how present-day German compares with Old English (as spoken before William the Conqueror arrived in 1066), which I studied as part of my English degree, many years ago. I didn't really need to use the language to communicate, but the project has taken on a life of its own, and now I do!

Tips for language learners

First, exposure! By this I mean listening to and reading the language in a realistic context as much as possible, even if it's only ten minutes a day. Second, use it as much as possible, by speaking and also some sort of written communication. In a way, learning a language is like taking up a sport – the theory and explanations are fine but you have to practise over and over again to be able to actually do it, and then keep practising to maintain it. New technologies have made it much easier – there are online courses, dictionaries that let you hear the pronunciation of a new word, spoken and written news online, Skype and similar platforms, the list is long. This leads me to the third piece of advice: give it time. You'll need to spend time on learning the language, and to allow yourself time before arriving at your goal.

A humorous anecdote

In Israel, soon after moving there, I went to a rather trendy café and asked for the drinks (in Hebrew, 'shtiya') list, but unfortunately got it wrong and said 'shtuyot' (rubbish). The waiter icily informed me that they didn't serve rubbish ...

105 Ffion's story

I'm 75 and Welsh, British, Spanish and European! I've been retired for some time, but worked for many years in the field of English language teaching and examining, teaching, running courses and working as a consultant. My parents were Welsh, though I actually grew up in Liverpool. I left home after finishing school, kicked around Cardiff and Bristol, fetched up in Mallorca, had a couple of kids, and worked my way through various Open University courses before settling in Cambridge by accident. I've enjoyed the city very much as a base for over 47 years. I worked for a well-known language school for nearly 30 years, then freelanced for a further 17, until sickness put paid to my gallivanting at the age of 71.

The languages in my life

I speak Welsh, English, French and Spanish and I can understand and read Italian and Catalan. Now I'm retired, everything I do is for pleasure. I read, listen to news, watch films and communicate with friends in all these languages. English is my main language because I live in England and because it's predominant in so many spheres.

I learnt Welsh at home and in chapel with my parents and relatives up to the age of five. I learnt English through 'Listen with Mother' – a radio programme for very little pre-school kids. I sang nursery rhymes, one involving marching the Grand Old Duke of York up to the top of the hill and down again many times. Learning English continued with English playmates and in primary school.

I learnt French through grammar-translation methodology in secondary school between the ages of 11 to 18. The lessons weren't much fun but French was chic and bohemian, I thought, and threw myself into the literature and the movies, the coffee and the cigarettes.

I've learnt a lot through living and/or working in the various countries. So a spell picking grapes near Bordeaux supplied daily if not incessant vocabulary school had overlooked to teach in seven long years.

What I enjoy about learning languages

I enjoy access to various views of the world and cross-cultural friendships. Literature and movies in their original languages are also pleasurable.

The most helpful thing is to spend time with kids who speak the language. Their spontaneous play and direct communications make everything easy to grasp. If you don't have kids to hand, watch kids' programmes on TV. You can start with programmes for the very youngest and work up the age groups and, of course, the language levels.

An ongoing project

Recently I've developed an acute nostalgia for Welsh and am actively studying it to improve my fluency and extend my vocabulary. I've addicted myself to a soap opera so I'm guaranteed 30 minutes listening comprehension of modern, informal language every day.

Tips for language learners

Find the things you enjoy in the language, the whole, real language not textbook-edited language samples. They try to make things easier for you by 'simplifying' but really make it harder with their focus on form when we humans like to focus on meaning. For example, listen to songs – you can get the lyrics (and translations) off the internet. How many times will you listen to and sing a song you love?

Take advantage of the media, traditional and new, and mostly free. For example, recording stuff onto your TV. You have the option of getting programmes with subtitles in either the original language or in your first language and the options of recording them to rewatch with or without the subtitles. Or, for example, watch the news in your own language so you know what the main stories are, then watch a later bulletin in the language you're learning. You'll be amazed at how much you understand. And if you do it again tomorrow and the day after, you'll be amazed at how quickly it gets easier and easier as so much of our everyday language use is constantly reusing the same lexis.

Another thing I'm currently enjoying enormously and finding useful is listening to an audio book of a modern Italian novel read beautifully in Italian while I'm simultaneously reading the English translation.

If you listen to lots of different speakers, you may find there's one that you feel you would particularly like to sound like. You can choose who you'd like to sound like – actor, news reader or DJ, for example.

A humorous anecdote

Present for the teacher?
A sweet little girl brings a cake. She says, 'It's made of my mother.'

106 Odogwu's story

I'm 80 and Nigerian. I was born in Nigeria into a Christian family and lived there during my formative years. Since then, I've lived in Canada for more than half of my life.

I got my first degree from a university in Nigeria. I was an undergraduate when the civil war broke out, and outside the country at the onset of the war, but I went back in the midst of the war to be with my family. War is an experience I would not wish even for an enemy. However, the experience will never be lost on me.

The languages in my life

I speak four languages. Igbo is my native tongue and English was the official language in Nigeria when I grew up. I speak to my extended family and Nigerian friends and associates in Igbo, and in Canada I speak English to my family and to everyone else in my community.

My undergraduate degree was in Romance languages, with French as my major and Spanish as minor at university in Nigeria. I also studied at the Université de Dakar in Senegal and the Université de Toulouse, France. At a certain period, I spoke both French and Spanish fluently and wrote my Master's degree thesis in French. I also studied Latin up to advanced level and loved Latin. The closest language to Latin is Italian; unfortunately, I haven't learnt to speak Italian.

I worked as a broadcaster at the Nigeria Broadcasting Corporation French Service and also taught French in high school, and at the University of Alberta, Canada as a sessional lecturer.

What I enjoy about learning languages

I most enjoy learning and being able to communicate in many languages, which throws the world wide open and removes many obstacles.

Tips for language learners

There's a lot to gain in being able to speak as many languages as possible. You have to believe in yourself, work hard at it and practise, practise, practise speaking the language. If possible, spend some time in the place or country where the language is spoken; that's the fastest way.

A humorous anecdote

I became a linguist by fluke rather than by design. When I was in primary school, as a Catholic, I was asked to learn to serve at Mass. During those days, priests said Mass in Latin; consequently, to be a server, one memorised the servers' responses as the priest went through the stages of the service, without even having any understanding of what one was reciting. I was intrigued by the solemnity of Latin, a language that made the server feel 'closer to God', or so we thought. When I grew up and was admitted into university to study French, I realised that a lot goes into studying foreign languages. We learnt the French 'vulgar expressions' first!

107 Mary's story

I'm 80. I was born in England and English is my first language. I also have Canadian citizenship and consider myself Canadian.

The languages in my life

I studied French and Latin throughout secondary school and university in England, apart from a mandatory immersion period at a French university. After university, I earned my teaching qualification, after which, throughout a long teaching career in Nigeria, England and Canada, I taught French as a second language to students from 12 to 18 years of age. The only time I taught Latin was during my teaching practice but knowledge of the language has been valuable in many ways. I used Latin socially on one occasion many years ago when there was no other common language. Since retirement, I haven't been able to speak French as often as I would like as I live in an Anglophone part of Canada, but I belong to a French-speaking group that meets once a month and I try to read and listen to French almost every day.

I've learnt six languages in all, though I don't speak all of them as well as I speak English and French. While still at university I met my husband, who's from Nigeria, and picked up some Igbo from him and his friends. We moved to Nigeria shortly after our graduation and there I learnt more of the language. At one point when my husband was away, our children and I stayed with his family in his home village where many of the inhabitants, especially the women, spoke no English. It was the perfect immersion environment. The basics of Igbo aren't difficult to grasp but the pronunciation is extremely tricky as it's a tonal language so there are many opportunities for making mistakes that range from mildly amusing to insulting and rude. My listening skills were good and I would say I was functional orally. Since I left Nigeria many years ago, my ability to speak and understand Igbo has faded through lack of frequent use, though I still use it in social situations.

The next language I learnt was German. One summer when I was a student I had ridden my bicycle around Germany with a friend who spoke basic German. I found the language interesting and thought I might like to learn it one day. A few years later, when I was living in Nigeria, I was visited by two German Reverend Fathers and mentioned my interest in learning their language. Their response was that I was much too old to learn another language. I was 24! There and then I decided I would definitely learn German one day! Eventually, two decades later, I was able to take beginner and intermediate level evening classes and became quite functional in the language.

After I retired, I took Spanish classes also at the beginner and intermediate level and, as with German, I became functional. I took Spanish because I enjoy learning in general and find languages interesting. The classes were also a social occasion.

My German has faded away over the years as I've had no opportunity to use it but I'm still able to read in Spanish and speak a little. I feel that should I wish or need to I could easily bring my level in both languages back to where it was.

What I enjoy about learning languages

I enjoy the sense of accomplishment in learning languages. I also enjoy the challenge. I'm quite a social person, so learning a number of languages has given me opportunities to interact with people of different cultures.

An ongoing project

At present, I'm working on improving my Igbo to bring it back to or above the level I was at years ago. I'm using books and the internet to relearn vocabulary and brush up on grammar. I practise in social situations when I have the opportunity. My husband and I speak mostly in English to each other but I practise on him from time to time.

Tips for language learners

I would advise language learners to take classes, learn the basics thoroughly, get some immersion, not be afraid of making mistakes, and practise, practise, practise!

A humorous anecdote

Here is an example of a mistake I made recently. My husband, who is a good cook, recently decided to make a Nigerian soup. This is part of our conversation as we ate:

Me (speaking in Igbo): The soup is delicious!
Husband (replying in English): It tastes like mud???

Key points

In this section, you have had the opportunity to read the case studies of successful language learners and the roles foreign languages have played and continue to play in their lives. Here are some key points to remember:

- In the target language, find what really motivates you ... football? fashion? history?
- Learn a lot of vocabulary by heart to kick-start communication.
- Study little and often.
- Get as much exposure as you can, reading and listening.
- Use technology.
- Find a tandem partner.
- If possible, spend time in a country where the target language is spoken.
- Practise, practise, practise.
- Remember you don't need to be perfect.
- Be patient and believe in yourself.
- Fall in love with a native speaker ...
- Anyone anywhere can learn a foreign language.

My own take-home notes on Tips from successful language learners

....

....

....

....

....

....

....

....

....

Conclusion

Congratulations on reaching the end of the book, or perhaps you've skipped to the conclusion as a short cut ...

Whatever your own individual circumstances, we hope we've inspired you to start or continue language learning. We've tried to show you that there is no one best way to learn a language – there are many different approaches and it's a matter of finding what works best for you. You'll probably find it most appropriate to mix and match to suit your own circumstances and needs. There's an amazing wealth of resources to help you and we hope we've been able to point you in some useful directions. For any language, there's masses of good material online to read and listen to and much of it is freely available.

But there's no getting around the fact that learning a language involves regular effort and a lot of exposure to the language. Adverts that promise you can become fluent in a new language in a few weeks are unlikely to live up to this promise. And don't forget that even a little progress is an achievement. You can get a lot of satisfaction from ordering a meal or booking a hotel room in the language you're learning. It's well worth putting in the effort for the pleasure that you will gain. The more you achieve, the more you will benefit from the new views of the world that another language can lead you to.

Finally, we'd like to remind you of some core points to remember as take-home messages.

Seven ways to become a successful language learner

1 Do it! Throw yourself in and begin a language learning adventure.

2 Do it often. Regular time slots for language learning and practice will produce the best results.

3 Set realistic goals. Small achievable aims will help you keep motivated.

4 Be a reflective learner. Plan, act and assess your progress frequently; adjust your approach if necessary.

5 Keep a balance. Words are the core of a language, but don't lose sight of grammar.

6 Spice it up. Keep your learning and practice activities varied, make sure it's fun.

7 Keep it up! Practise as much as you can; you're sure to have a break in your routine sometimes but don't let that stop you getting back into it as soon as you can.

We hope that your language learning will bring you as much pleasure as it's brought us and the many inspiring people we've spoken to in the course of writing this book.

Anyone anywhere can learn a foreign language.

References

Here are a few of the many fascinating books on language and language learning aimed at the general reader. Perhaps you'd like to dip into or read some of them?

Aitchison, J. (2012). *Words in the Mind: An Introduction to the Mental Lexicon* (4th edn). Chichester: Wiley Blackwell.

Brandreth, G. (2018). *Have You Eaten Grandma?* London: Penguin Books.

Crystal, D. (2010). *The Cambridge Encyclopedia of Language* (3rd edn). Cambridge: Cambridge University Press.

Crystal, D. (2019). *The Cambridge Encyclopedia of the English Language* (3rd edn). Cambridge: Cambridge University Press.

Dent, S. (2020). *Word Perfect: Etymological Entertainment For Every Day of the Year*. London: John Murray Press.

Kohn, M. (2019). *Four Words for Friend: Why Using More Than One Language Matters Now More Than Ever*. New Haven: Yale University Press.

Lightbown, P. M. and Spada, N. (2013). *How Languages are Learned* (3rd edn). Oxford: Oxford University Press.

McCarthy, M. (2017). *English Grammar: Your Questions Answered*. Cambridge: Prolinguam Publishing.

Pinker, S. (1995). *The Language Instinct: How the Mind Creates Language*. London: Penguin Science.

The books listed below are just some of the more specialised books we have drawn on both during our careers and in writing this book.

Batstone, R. (ed.) (2010). *Sociocognitive Perspectives on Language Use and Language Learning*. Oxford: Oxford University Press.

Benson, P. and Voller, P. (1997). *Autonomy and Independence in Language Learning*. London: Pearson Education.

Cohen, A. D. and Macaro, E. (eds) (2007). *Language Learner Strategies: Thirty Years of Research and Practice*. Oxford: Oxford University Press.

Ellis, G. and Sinclair, B. (1989). *Learning to Learn English: A Course in Learner Training*. Cambridge: Cambridge University Press.

Ellis, R. (1994). *The Study of Second Language Acquisition*. Oxford: Oxford University Press.

Ellis, R. (2015). *Understanding Second Language Acquisition* (2nd edn). Oxford: Oxford University Press.

Koda, K. (2005). *Insights into Second Language Reading: A Cross-Linguistic Approach*. Cambridge: Cambridge University Press.

O'Malley, M. and Chamot, A. U. (1995). *Learning Strategies in Second Language Acquisition*. Cambridge: Cambridge University Press.

Schmitt, N. and McCarthy, M. (eds) (1997). *Vocabulary*. Cambridge: Cambridge University Press.

Scollon, R., Wong Scollon, S. and Jones, R. H. (2012). *Intercultural Communication: A Discourse Approach* (3rd edn). Chichester: Wiley Blackwell.

Skehan, P. (1998). *A Cognitive Approach to Language Learning*. Oxford: Oxford University Press.

Watts, R. J. (2003). *Politeness*. Cambridge: Cambridge University Press.

Acknowledgements

We would both like to thank Alison Silver our editor, in particular for her enthusiasm, precision and project management skills in bringing the book into being. We're also very grateful to our designer Bob Swan for transforming our manuscript into an attractive book and his help with the publishing process with Amazon, and Peter Bull for his stylish illustrations.

We would also like to thank Anita Pincas, who led the MA TESOL programme we followed together at the Institute of Education, University College London and whose organisational skills, encouragement and enthusiasm were an inspiration. We are very grateful to Henry Widdowson, who headed up that excellent MA programme. The Institute emphasised the importance of practice being based on sound research-informed theory and this provided our motivation for writing this book.

Felicity would like to thank her school and university language teachers – in particular Martin Weir, Lilian Ross, Margaret Pirie and James Forsyth – who gave her a love of languages that has determined the course of both her professional and personal life. She would also like to thank Michael McCarthy, with whom she has co-written a number of books on vocabulary, for all that she has learnt from him about language and about writing.

Patricia would like to thank her teachers at grammar school: Ken Byrne, who was an inspiring French teacher with a pleasant yet rigorous approach, and Brian Lewis, whose Latin grammar instruction was a great help when she began learning German later in life at a time when grammar was out of fashion! She would like to thank her former boss and friend Professor Aline Gohard-Radenovic for her support and encouragement in her teaching and research, as well as friends and former colleagues Patricia Kohler and Gaby Probst for their help with the French and German in the book.

We are both also indebted to the colleagues with whom we have worked and the many people we have taught over the years; we have learnt a great deal about language learning from them.

We owe particular thanks to John Meed for his advice on self-publishing and to Rosalie Kerr for her constructive comments on our manuscript. Finally, we wish to thank the language learners who contributed the case studies illustrating their experiences and offering their own tips.

About the authors

Felicity O'Dell has loved language learning since she was a child. Having studied French, German and Latin at school, she went on to do Russian, with subsidiary French, at university. She has also taught herself some basic Italian and Spanish along the way. She has a PhD in Soviet education (focusing on the use of reading to teach moral values to primary school children) and a Master's in Education specialising in Teaching English to Speakers of Other Languages (TESOL). She started out teaching modern languages in a UK secondary school but has spent most of her career teaching English to adult learners with a wide range of work and language backgrounds. While working at a language school in Cambridge in the UK for many years she was responsible for the self-access learning centre, which involved helping learners improve their independent learning skills. Her late and sorely missed husband was Russian and that was the language they spoke at home. She has written many books for language learners and has travelled widely in the UK and abroad leading workshops and giving talks at teachers' conferences. She has also worked as a consultant for various organisations, including the BBC, LT123 and several international examination boards.

Patricia Pullin enjoyed learning languages at school, beginning French when she was eight and later continuing with Italian and Latin. She also started learning German as an adult and is still working on it! She studied English literature at university before doing a Master's in Education, specialising in Teaching English to Speakers of Other Languages (TESOL). She also has a PhD in Applied Linguistics based on research into workplace communication amongst native speakers of English and speakers of English as a lingua franca. She has lived for most of her adult life in Switzerland, where she taught English initially in adult education and later in higher education. She was a member of a multilingual team at the bilingual University of Fribourg/Freiburg, providing specialised courses for the Faculty of Economics. Subsequently, she was Head of English at the University of Zurich / ETH Language Center, where she worked with a team of teachers on the development of specialised courses for staff and students in different academic disciplines. Over recent years, she has co-taught interdisciplinary courses in Germany and Switzerland on using English as a medium of instruction in non-English-speaking universities.

Felicity and Patricia met at the Institute of Education in London when they were both studying for the MA in TESOL.

If you liked this book, the authors would be very grateful if you could review the book on Amazon so that more readers can enjoy it and also become successful language learners. As independent authors, our readers' views are very important to us. Thank you!

My *Success in Language Learning* Notes

My *Success in Language Learning* Notes

My *Success in Language Learning* Notes

My *Success in Language Learning* Notes

My *Success in Language Learning* Notes

An ideal practical introduction for even the most reluctant language learner and a perfect practical guide for language learners at all levels. A great piece of work.

DAVID CRYSTAL, author of the *Cambridge Encyclopedia of Language*

Printed in Great Britain
by Amazon

82804613R00153